THE BOOK OF

Scripture

vs.

Culture

Pastor Raymond Vietmeier

ISBN 978-1-0980-2288-4 (paperback)
ISBN 978-1-0980-2821-3 (hardcover)
ISBN 978-1-0980-2289-1 (digital)

Christian Faith Publishing, Inc.
832 Park Avenue
Meadville, PA 16335
www.christianfaithpublishing.com

All statements made about political parties and persons in those parties have been aired on nation-wide and/or world-wide television broadcasts or printed in newspapers. There is nothing written herein that the public was not previously been made aware. They have been mentioned as a reminder of the truth.

Printed in the United States of America

CHAPTER 1

An Explanation and the Purpose for This Book

The paragraph you are now reading is the result of God wanted me, the author, to make a point very clear to the readers of this book. At various times I will state that this book is God inspired. I need to clarify that those parts of the book that talk about people and events in my life God may have suggested I include them, but the sentences used are not inspired in detail by God. The wording used is from my own memory plus may even be modified by the editor to sound better. Those parts of the book where I am comparing what God has inspired in his scriptures, vs the paths that our country's culture is taking is inspired by God down to the exact wording used. God did not want the readers to think that one hundred percent of this book was God inspired down to the exact wording of every sentence. Only certain parts are truly God inspired sentences. The fact that this book is to be published is God's desire. He directed me, as one of many of his prophets, to write it so that his words to the people get printed and published for all to read. God uses his prophets to get his words out to the people including those words that may foretell what will happen in the future under certain circumstances.

The name of this book describes its primary purpose. That is, to get God's word out about his concern as to what his planned paths are for his people as they are written in the scriptures of the Holy Bible verses the paths being taken by our current culture in the United States and all around the world. Christians are taught that

God has given we humans a free will. We can choose to listen to God and allow him to guide us down the path he has planned for us or we can ignore him and listen to Satan and go down a path that will lead us to eternal damnation rather than eternal life.

Secondary to that main purpose this book will show how he takes a selected individual and guides him down the path that he has planned for him since before creation. You heard correctly. God has an overall plan for the entire world which is supplemented by his plan for each individual. It is believed by most biblical scholars that both plans were designed by God even before he created the universe, the earth and the people, animals and plants which occupy the earth.

The Bible also teaches us that we are not to love the world. The world we are not to love is the dark world which is under the control of Satan. We are allowed to love the world as God created it. That is, the mountains, flowers, rivers, oceans as well as each other and the plants and animals he placed on the earth.

> Later you will find that Jesus taught us to love each other. The Bible teaches us that we humans are above the animals. I now quote Mathew 6:25-27:
>
> Therefore I tell you, do not worry about your life, what you will eat or drink; or about your body, what you will wear. Is not life more than Food, and the body more than clothes? Look at the birds of the air; they do not sow or reap or store away in barns, yet your heavenly Father feeds them.
>
> Are you not much more valuable then they. Can any one of you by worrying add a single hour to your life?

We have preservation societies which continue to see that the population of animals all over the world are cared for and great attempts are in place to assure their continued existence and their continued health.

However, the world we are not to be in love with is the dark world. This is explained quite eloquently in the words of Jesus in the biblical scripture of John 15:18–25:

> If the world hates you, keep in mind that it hates me first. If you belonged to the world, it would love you as its own. As it is, you do not belong to the world, but I have chosen you out of the world. That is why the world hates you. Remember what I told you. A servant is not greater than his master. If they persecuted me, they will persecute you also. If they obeyed my teaching they will obey yours also. They will treat you this way because of my name, for they do not know the one who sent me. If I had not come and spoken to them, they would not be guilty of sin; but now they have no excuse for their sin. Whoever hates me hates my Father as well. If I had not done among them the works no one else did, they would not be guilty of sin. As it is, they have seen and yet they have hated both me and my Father. But this is to fulfill what is written in their Law. They hated me without reason.

In the Bible, Jesus has this to say in John 12:35–36:

> Then Jesus told them, "You are going to have the light just a little while longer. Walk while you have the light, before darkness over-takes you. Whoever walks in the dark does not know where they are going. Believe in the light while you have the light, so that you may become children of light."

Because those who live in the dark do not know where they are going, they are blinded and unable to see the truth like those who live in the light. One common belief of those who live in the dark is that Moses did not write the first four books of the Bible. Jesus rebukes that idea in John 5:45–47:

> But do not think I will accuse you before the Father. Your accuser is Moses, on whom your hopes are set. If you believed Moses, you would believe me, for he wrote about me. But since you do not believe what he wrote, how are you going to believe what I say?

Scripture also says that those who live in the dark think that all the things believed by those who live in the light are foolishness, for example, those who say the Bible is foolishness because it was not written by God or any higher being and was simply written by men. One only has to read from 1 Corinthians 2:14:

> The person without the Spirit does not accept the things that come from the Spirit of God but considers them foolishness, and cannot understand them because they are discerned only through the Spirit.

As we see the culture within the United States turning toward the dark world, we stand to no longer be blessed by God. It is written that the nation that accepts God is blessed by God. But the nation that no longer accepts God will no longer be blessed by God. The new dark culture led by the Democratic Party here in the United States wants to remove all mention of God from all government buildings and public places. They do not like the wording of "In God We Trust" written on our currency. They do not like the Ten Commandments to exist in our courthouses. Yet it is the courts that try to teach us not to break any of the Ten Commandments. How can that make any sense? It simply is not logical.

Sadly, the current culture in most of the world is made up of those who live in the dark. Therefore, there are now those who want a culture where babies are murdered because mothers do not want them. A news report just came out that the governors of the states of New York and Illinois just signed a bill into law that the lives of babies can be terminated at or shortly after birth.

Those who live in the light know that God places the spirit He selects into the embryo at the time of conception, that is, at the exact time when one little sperm enters the egg. Therefore, life begins immediately upon conception. As was stated earlier, the culture of those who live in the dark world sees the concept of life beginning at the time of conception as more foolishness.

So many good people who consider themselves Christians believe that if God is a loving God, He will allow all to enter heaven if they feel they are a good person and treat others in a kind fashion. Jesus makes it very clear in John 14:6:

> I am the way and the truth and the life. No one comes to the Father except through me.

He adds to that in verse 7:

> If you really know me, you will know my Father as well from now on, you do know him and have seen him.

Some believe because they have regularly attended a Christian church, they are a true Christian. Some say because their parents were Christians, that makes them Christians as well.

See Jesus's answers in His teaching of Nicodemus in John 3:3–7:

> "Very truly I tell you, no one can see the kingdom of God unless they are born again."

"How can someone be born when they are old?" Nicodemus asked. "Surely they cannot enter a second time into their mother's womb to be born!"

Jesus answered, "Very truly I tell you, no one can enter the kingdom of God unless they are born of water and the Spirit. Flesh gives birth to flesh, but the Spirit gives birth to spirit. You should not be surprised at my saying, 'You must be born again.'"

Before continuing, the author wishes to acknowledge that all biblical quotes are from the New International Version (NIV) Study Bible unless otherwise stated.

We are to sincerely, without question, love God! The best biblical quote for this is Matthew 22:37–40:

To answer the lawyer's question, Jesus quoted from the great Jewish confession of faith called the Shema. The confession is called this because it begins with the Hebrew word, "Love the Lord your God with all your heart with all your soul, and with all your mind." This is the first and great commandment. And the second is like it "You shall love your neighbor as yourself." On these two commandments hang all the Law and the Prophets. (NKJV)

As stated earlier, the secondary purpose is to show how God selects some individuals and then guides and directs them down his planned path in order for them to be trained to ultimately do special assignments for him. Chapters 2 through 5 are concerned with this.

Chapter 2 will tell about one such individua from the time he was a small child until he became a man and began to work for God as a pastor, disciple and prophet.

Chapter 3 will tell about how God protected that same individual from harm and even death so that his plan for that person would eventually come to be fulfilled.

Chapter 4 deals with the lessons this selected individual learned as it relates to his lifelong relationship with God.

Then, Chapter 5 describes what lessons the person learned as a Pastor about scripture vs culture. Primarily, how the writing of sermons under the directions of God became a major part of the person's training.

Chapters 6 and 7 describe how God used the persons Spiritual Gift of musical talent to write songs for him. These are God's songs but he directed this person to write and produce CDs so these songs can teach those who listen to them about what God wants them to learn and know; primarily, the truth and not the lies of the dark world. The theme of each song describs the truth for all to hear.

Beginning with chapter 8 this book will tell about the need for disciples in order to pass on to as many people about the gospels; that God sent his only Son Jesus to earth to become the Lamb of God and pay the ultimate price in order to pay for the sins of those who accept Jesus and decide to be born again and follow Jesus and his teachings. The main function of these last 3 chapters is to tell the truth about God's concern for how our culture is leaning toward the dark world and not following God's instructions as written in the scriptures of the Holy Bible. The story begins when the boy was very young but continues through the boy's life until he was a grown man when God spoke to him directly so that he would obey God as he began to do God's work as God directed. Each task provided more of God's guidance and directing to cause the person to do God's work in the precise way God wanted. This chapter gives a personal life history of this anointed one to whom God was teaching there were more things to learn. Therefore, this book will cover the specific ways God taught this person. It explains what lessons the person learned as the result of various assignments given to him by God.

God accomplished His plan for this person by guidance and training. Ultimately, the boy became a man and must begin using the guidance and training God provided throughout his life.

In another chapter, this book tells of the miracles God performed in order to keep this person protected from harm and even death multiple times. These miracles began during childhood and continued throughout his life. You will see how this person learned simply because of his very close and loving relationship with the Holy Trinity. Keep in mind what was quoted earlier about the two commands in the Jewish confession of faith called the Shema about loving God with all your heart, soul, and mind. Throughout this boy's life, he continued to do exactly that. He always kept God first—not only God the Father but the Son and the Holy Spirit.

These are the lessons the person learned both as God ordained and finally as an ordained independent minister through a fellowship which is authorized by Matthew 28:19–20. One assignment from God was as a pastor to preach to a special congregation for God.

There are the lessons when God had this person write songs for Him. They were God's songs, and God provided the melodies and guided the person to the scriptures to use as the source of the lyrics of each song.

God then had new songs He wanted to be produced, but this time the topics or sources of the lyrics were to be accomplished as though the songwriter was researching for the writing of sermons.

Finally, God wants this book to tell about the need for disciples.

The Story of a Boy Who Was Guided through Life by God

This chapter and the next one were the most difficult chapters to write. Chapter 2 tells a brief story of my life—the author. The next chapter is similar because it tells about the miracles God performed in order to guide me down the paths He planned for me so that I would learn what I needed to know in order to do the work I must perform for Him.

The first reason for the difficulty is that I wanted to explain how God takes certain chosen people and then guides and directs them to go down the path that He has planned. The second reason is that this book is about the comparison of scriptures vs. cultures of the dark world. How does one insert one's life story and God's miracles, yet somehow have it tied into the main theme of scripture vs. culture? Hopefully, you will be able to recognize those events that took place which allowed me to learn about how many cultures, including that of our own country, are diametrically opposed to what God has in mind in His inspired writing of the Bible.

God has two kinds of paths. The first is the path He wants for His entire creation. The second are the paths He plans for each individual in order to get each of us to do as He wishes. There are some, like myself, who have been assigned a path which will allow them to become preachers and disciples. We are the ones God wants to prune and train so that eventually we will be fully prepared to do His work.

I wanted to write a brief version of the primary things in my life that only I know but have a direct relationship to God's plan for me. To try to tell the life story about anyone else is impossible. I do not have the knowledge about the life of anyone else to the degree that is required to write their life's story. The only life story that I can write about is my own. I finally decided to use my real name and not a pseudonym. I also have written my story in the third person so as to make sure I was not the center of attention. It was my intent to keep from writing an autobiography. The story must be centered on how God guided and directed me all through my life. As the author, I did not want to draw attention to myself but rather to God. Therefore, the story does not contain every detail about my life but only a summary which pertains to God's guidance and the places where scripture is compared to culture.

You may be wondering why a story about the author's life is included in a book about scripture vs. culture. Here is the logic behind my decision to include this chapter. Please remember God had a plan for me to become a preacher and enlighten those who would listen about Jesus—the gospel. I was to also write a book primarily about scripture vs. culture. That could only be accomplished if I was guided and trained by God all through my life to eventually prepare me for my multiple assignments to do His work and tell others about what is going wrong with our culture. I am to point out why our culture is becoming the complete opposite of what the scriptures teach us. I would no longer work for companies in a world under the control of Satan. I was to be one of God's children—His children of light. Then it was God's plan for me to become more than one of His children. I was to become an ordained preacher. That thought did not enter my human brain until I became an elderly adult.

Remember what Jesus says in the book of John 12:35:

> Then Jesus told them, You are going to have the light just a little while longer. Walk while you have the light, before the darkness overtakes you.

Whoever walks in the dark does not know where they are going.

Also in the book of Romans 2:19–21:

> If you are convinced that you are a guide for the blind, a light for those who are in the dark, an instructor of the foolish, a teacher of little children, because you have in the law the embodiment of knowledge and truth—you, then, who teaches others, do you not teach yourself?

Ephesians 5:8–11 states:

> For you were once darkness, but now you are light in the Lord. Live as children of light for the fruit of the light consists of all goodness, righteousness and truth, find out what pleases the Lord. Have nothing to do with the fruitless deeds of darkness but rather expose them.

These verses from the Holy Bible teach us that we who live in the light must also see the light as well. But as for those who live in the dark world and do not know where they are going, we are to *expose them.*

Therefore, according to Jesus, we must live in the light as children of light because it is only those whom God considers His own—who are the children of light—who will see the kingdom of heaven. The children of light can enter heaven because upon being born again, they became one of many children of light. However, Jesus cautions the children of light about failing to be fruitful, about obeying His commands as He obeyed God's commands. Jesus told us in John 15:1–17 about this warning. If we, who are children of light, fail to be fruitful, we will be cut from Jesus, the vine, and thrown down to wither. Then, such branches are thrown into the fire to be

l. I am not exaggerating this one bit. That means that those who are not fruitful and fail to obey Jesus's commands will no longer be in Jesus and Jesus will no longer be in them. They are cut from Jesus, the vine.

So we remain children of light because we grow as Christians. To grow as Christians, we become fruitful, and we also must continue to obey Jesus's commands. Additionally, we must expose all those who are in the dark according to the above quote from the book of Ephesians. This book exposes those who live in the dark and act in complete disobedience to the teachings of the Bible. To them, the Bible, God, and Jesus are all foolishness.

It is easy to see this battle going on in the world with the radicalized haters of everyone but their own. What seems to be so ironic to me is the fact that they think anyone who is not radicalized as they are must die because that is what God wants. We are told by those who are Muslims that the Koran does not talk about Muslims killing other Muslims. Nor does it say Muslims should kill Christians and Jews. In fact, we are told, and I believe them, that they are not to kill anyone. Remember "Thou shall not kill" is one of the Ten Commandments. God said that vengeance is His and His alone.

Before I begin the actual story, I wish to explain that from the time I was old enough to begin to understand what my life was about, I understood that I had a very close relationship with God and His Son, Jesus. It was not until the end of my story that I fully realized that my entire life I was guided by God to eventually work for Him as a singer, songwriter, musician, minister, preacher, author, and even a landscape artist painting pictures which express scriptures. At some point, I realized I was planned to be *God ordained* and eventually be ordained by a Christian fellowship that recognized I was already God ordained and had the biblical knowledge to be ordained by them under the authority of Matthew 28:19–20. After answering several hours of questions and having those answers reviewed by a council of elders, I was officially an *ordained independent minister*—in more common terms, a nondenominational preacher.

And now, for the life story of a boy who was chosen by God to do His work, the story begins with the boy being born Raymond Junior McDowell into a dysfunctional family. Raymond's birth mother was an alcoholic, and his biological father was a womanizer and abusive to his mother and two sisters as well as Raymond. Ray does not remember being abused, but later in life he was informed by one of his sisters who is only two years older that all three children were abused at the hands of their father. Raymond remembers being in their apartment unattended by anyone because his mother worked in a factory in St. Louis.

As it turned out, his mother got paid one Friday and went to a bar and began to spend the rent and food money on booze. She got drunk and ended up in jail. Raymond was told later that she had been hiding with her three children in order to protect herself and her kids from the abusive treatment of their father. He did not know where his children were.

Had it not been for her ending up in jail, the hiding would have continued to be successful. As it was, their father knew many of the officers of the St. Louis Police Department. That Friday, the children were left alone in the apartment as usual, but with only one slice of bread. Raymond was only two at the time, and his next oldest sister was four, and his oldest sister was six. He did not have a chance to win the battle over that one slice of bread.

A neighbor in their apartment complex heard the three kids arguing and fighting over that slice of bread. She called the police and explained that the McDowell kids were fighting and their mother had not come home from work. The police knew that their mother was in jail and informed their father what was going on. He and the police broke into the apartment and "rescued his three children" as he later told Raymond. Raymond remembered that he did not know this man but that his two sisters did know him. They left the apartment with their father.

Raymond remembered there being a fire nearby with large fire hoses strewn all over the street and sidewalk. Because he was only two years old, he had a difficult time walking over the hoses. Their father picked Raymond up and slung him over his right arm with his right hand on his hip. Raymond's ribs were hurting, but he was too afraid to say anything. He only remembered his two sisters saying over and over, "She is a bad lady."

After that, their parents divorced. Raymond's birth mother remarried and moved to California. His father also remarried but to a woman who had an older boy from a previous marriage. She and her son were very abusive. Raymond remembers being afraid of both of them. He now has a picture taken with this very mean boy and his two sisters, sitting on a terrace. He still remembers the four posing for that picture. Many of you may not believe that a seventy-five-year-old man could possibly remember things that happened when he was only two years old. Like many, Raymond does have an excellent long-term memory. Sometimes though, he does forget where he puts things and has to search for them. Like many his age, he begins to have that problem.

Their father did not really want his three children. But he also did not want his ex-wife to have custody either. At some point, he sent all three to the Missouri Baptist Children's Home. Later, Raymond was sent to live with a farming family. His two sisters were sent to a Catholic orphanage.

This is where God began to take control in order for His plan for Raymond to be accomplished. He *had* to be removed from this dysfunctional family and put under the care of a true Christian family. God had to get many other people involved in order for this to happen.

Eventually, their father dear decided to put Raymond up for adoption. As he now looks back, he realizes that it might have been God Who wanted him out of that original family causing this adoption to take place. Either Raymond's father forged Raymond's mother's signature on the parental rights form or he had someone else forge her signature. One of his sisters wrote a letter to the boy's mother that "Little Raymond was being put up for adoption" and she wanted his mother to know.

In August of 1948, just one month before his fifth birthday, Raymond was adopted into a wonderful family. It took some time for him to adjust and understand that he now had a complete new set of parents, grandparents, aunts, uncles, and many first cousins. He even had a new name. His new parents took him to their church where he was baptized. His new mother's older brother, Raymond's Uncle Harry, was appointed as his godfather. He would also have a new name with his godfather's first name as his new middle name—hence Raymond Harry Vietmeier.

It would be some time before his birth mother could come to St. Louis to see about regaining custody of her little boy. The Division of Family Services told her he was already adopted into a fine Christian family and was doing very well. He was loved and cared for. She was told that with her problem with alcoholism and obvious poor parenting skills, the boy was better off with his new family. She was told that it would be best to leave things as they were.

Raymond was so used to being called Raymond that he had a hard time adjusting to the fact that his new family preferred to call him Ray. He would respond with "My name is Raymond, not Ray."

As a young boy, Ray often sang "Jesus Loves Me" over and over. He sang that song even when he was supposed to be taking a nap. Somehow he always knew that he had a very close relationship with the Holy Trinity. Ray thought everybody did. He was used to being around those who were children of light, especially those in his new family.

His Uncle Harry belonged to the same denomination as Ray's parents but attended a different church. His church had many social events such as ice-cream socials, watermelon socials, and even a wonderful Christmas pageant each year. He was always invited by his Uncle Harry to join in with his immediate family and attend these events. Ray loved spending a few days with his Uncle Harry's family which included his first cousin Cheryl.

God would now guide him, direct him, and train him in order to prepare him to do His work. Ray and his new parents attended church every Sunday. At first, Ray attended Sunday school and began to learn the stories in the Bible. He joined the youth choir. At the age of accountability, he began the two years of confirmation classes and was born again one Palm Sunday. That means he joined the church as a full member of the congregation taking communion as an adult. He no longer went to Sunday school but attended church services.

God needed Ray to become involved and take part in the battle between good and evil going on in the entire world. It is also going on in our own country and in our own minds. The good side is based on the scriptures in the Holy Bible. The evil side is the cultures of much of the world. Those who believe in the teachings of the Bible are in a constant battle with those who live in the dark world, guided by the evil one.

As part of God's overall plan for Ray, He gave him the gift of musical talent. Even upon first being adopted, his parents gave him plastic toy instruments, and he could play songs by ear within a matter of minutes with each one of those plastic toys. When Ray was nine years old, his parents decided to enroll him in formal music lessons. He did not realize it at the time, but this was part of God's plan for him. God knew that eventually he would assign Ray to be a music minister. Then when Ray would later be ordained and hold church services at places which had no music minister, he would have to perform both duties.

Here is a brief description of what took place in Ray's life that involved honing his musical talent in order to prepare for what was to eventually happen. Shortly after starting his formal music training, Ray performed on a local St. Louis radio station. At age fourteen, he began writing songs and performed on a local television show. He was trained in music theory as well as playing many different instruments. He began with the accordion but played the tenor sax in both junior high and high school. Both piano and organ were next. Eventually, Ray learned to play eighteen different instruments.

At age fifteen, he became a member of the Ace Nash Symphony playing in both group and individual competitions. By age seventeen, he began teaching music at Ludwig Aeolian Studios in St. Louis. The piano and organ teacher was Mr. Olly Sandel who was also the organist for the St. Louis Cardinals at Busch Stadium. Olly like Ray even though he was much older. He liked Ray so much that when he had to play at the ballgames, he had the manager of the studio appoint Ray as his substitute teacher. Soon he substituted for drums, guitar, and, naturally, all woodwind instruments like the tenor sax.

Also, at age seventeen, he used his stage name and founded the Ray Scott Trio consisting of a drummer and slap bass player with Ray switching between the accordion and piano. He chose Ray Scott as his stage name because too many announcers could not pronounce Vietmeier. For your benefit, Ray's last name is pronounced as "Veetmeyer." The trio performed at private parties, including weddings, birthday parties, and many similar events. Neither Ray nor the trio ever became famous, but fame was not in his desires. Ray simply loved to play and teach music to others.

You are learning about all of this not to emphasize Ray's musical talent. It was God Who gave him that talent for multiple very good reasons. God wanted Ray to experience playing before people and even audiences of up to five thousand so he would not feel uneasy preaching before others. God needed him to become an accomplished musician, singer, or songwriter because those abilities would be needed later in life. It was all part of His plan for one individual. It was all meant to be training for what would be part of his many assignments to do God's work.

At age nineteen, the trio was dissolved, and Ray joined the Navy. While in the Navy, he sang at nightclubs overseas. When in his ship's home port of Long Beach, California, he joined an acting company and performed in two live plays. This was additional training for being before large audiences. He was not a very good actor. Ray did not really like the Hollywood style atmosphere and the liberal views of most actors. They did not seem to understand the importance of God and His inspired words of the Bible. It was not until now that he realized that many actors did as they pleased and were part of the dark world culture. Most of them seemed to hate anything to do with conservative points of view or even the mention of the Bible, God, or Jesus. His acting career was short, but he believed God wanted him to see what was going on in the dark world of our own country's culture.

As a singer, Ray was well received by audiences in every port his ship visited. In Hong Kong, his closest shipmates who knew about his singing talked to the management of the World of Suzie Wong nightclub. Ray was asked to sing for two hours. That was the place where the movie by that same name was filmed in the early 1960s. While serving in the Vietnam area, there was a miracle that will be covered in the next chapter on miracles God performed in order to keep Ray from harm so as to be able to eventually do His work for Him.

He joined the Navy for several reasons, but the most important reason was because he saw the war in Vietnam not as a civil war but a war against good and evil. Communism is evil because in order for communism to be successful, the people must not worship God or practice any form of religion. The leaders of the communist party and their government must be the people's god. Today, we see the Chinese government, the North Korean government, and other communist nations burning Christian churches, torturing Christian pastors, and burning Bibles.

Ray's father served in the Navy in World War II. Ray remembered what happened in that war when Germany and the Japanese attacked and occupied one island or one country at a time. Eventually, they planned to attack the United States. It is true that Hawaii was a territory and not a state yet. Likewise, Alaska was also just a territory, but the Japanese attacked both territories. Yes, few people know that two islands of the Alaskan Aleutian chain were occupied by Japan. They built airstrips and bunkers for large guns on those islands. They savagely attacked not only Pearl Harbor but the city of Honolulu killing civilians. They attacked Hickam Field, an Army Air Corps base in the mountains of the Hawaiian island of Oahu.

Ray saw wars in Korea and Vietnam as an attempt to follow the logic of the Japanese and gradually occupy one island or one country at a time until they were able to attack the United States. They took over Cuba in 1958 with the assistance of the Soviet Union. In Vietnam, the north was supplied weapons from a wide range of communist nations. Countries like the Soviet Union and China were the primary suppliers. That was his primary reason for joining the Navy. Ray wanted to help protect our own country which was founded under God and not a political party which required its people to worship the government and not God.

Venezuela is currently in complete chaos. When things began to fall apart at the hands of Pres. Hugo Chavez, he pleaded with the people to do away with the constitution and appoint him as a benevolent dictator. They foolishly did as he asked. Then things got worse. There is a new dictator now, but things are still in ruins. Venezuela is now occupied by Russian, Cuban, and even Iranian troops.

Our own President Obama made two statements that completely shocked many in this country. In one of his books, he praised Fidel Castro as being a hero. He also praised Hugo Chaves. He made the statement that he chose his friends very carefully. He said he especially admired those professors who advocated communism. Now we have the so-called Progressive Democrats waging war against President Trump like no other president has ever been attacked before in the history of our country. It is one witch hunt after another, and each time they fail because there is no foundation for such attacks. The false news media in the United States loves to report anything that is bad but refuses to report the good that the president and his party has accomplished. They call President Trump a racist, but Dr. Martin Luther King Jr.'s niece has come to President Trump's defense. She openly tells the truth about his policies helping any and all people of color. She reported on the Christian Broadcasting Network (CBN) that the Democrats are the same ones who caused all the trouble in the south and that they are the true racists. They formed the KKK. They made the laws about segregation all throughout the 1950s and 1960s. They were the cause of the revolution her uncle, Martin Luther King Jr., fought so hard against.

Getting back to Ray's training and guidance by God, about six months into the Navy, Ray resumed dating Darlene Jones from high school. They dated off and on but not steadily at first. On Christmas Eve of 1963, Ray invited Darlene to join him along with his mother's side of the family to celebrate Christmas Eve. While there, he proposed to her, and she said yes. Although this made it official, they had talked about marriage even while they were dating. On February 1, 1964, Ray and his fiancée, Darlene Jones, were married.

When Ray's ship was in port at Pearl Harbor in 1964, his bride joined him. Before her arrival though, Ray's very close friend and fellow shipmate, Keith Moller, who preferred to be called Rick for some reason, helped locate an inexpensive apartment for the young couple. Ray's ship was scheduled to stay in port for at least five months. They had little time together before Ray was shipped out. It had been several months between the time they were married and when she was scheduled to join Ray in Hawaii. Ray and his good friend Rick found a nice apartment within walking distance of Waikiki Beach.

Now for a special bit of humor, in college, Ray was taught that any written material should include at least two humorous events. It just so happens there were humorous events that took place while Ray's ship was in port at Pearl Harbor.

When Rick and Ray finally found the right apartment, they noticed that it was infested with roaches. The entire island of Oahu was filled with roaches ranging from small red ones to large three-inch-long black ones. Before Darlene's arrival, Rick and Ray went to stores to see what kind of spray or another device was best to get rid of the roaches from the apartment. They were told that nothing like that worked anymore. The roaches had become immune to all chemicals. They were told that they needed to get a gecko—yes, a lizard. Ray found one in the backyard and brought it into the apartment before his wife's arrival. He named it Fred for fun.

Darlene arrived in June of 1964, and Ray met her at the airport with one of his ship's official navy trucks. She loved the small studio apartment. One day while Ray was at work, Darlene called his office asking, "Guess what is on the kitchen faucet?"

"Oh, that must be Fred," Ray replied.

"Fred!" she yelled.

He quickly explained, "Well, in Hawaii, you either have to put up with thousands of roaches or a small lizard to keep the roach population in check."

She calmed down immediately and said, "I'll settle for Fred."

Darlene got a job at a shop across the street from the main entrance to Waikiki Beach. It specialized in bikinis, *mumus*, and *hulamus*. She was required to wear a different but very expensive *hulamu* each night. It was the boss's way of advertising for little money. That made going out to restaurants very enjoyable. Darlene just happened to be very beautiful, and wearing the most expensive Hawaiian attire only made her look fabulous.

While in port at Pearl Harbor, the very famous Hollywood actor, John Wayne, was filming his new movie In Harm's Way on Ford Island where Ray's ship was docked. It is a very large island in the middle of Pearl Harbor.

As one might imagine, many Navy wives would come on base frequently to see if they could see or even meet John Wayne in person. Because filming took place mostly on Ford Island, John Wayne and the entire movie crew had to use Ray's ship's fifty-foot liberty launches to go back and forth between Ford Island and the main base. One evening after work, Ray took one of the liberty launches to leave Ford Island to head home to the apartment. As Ray exited the boat and began walking up the ramp at the main base, a very tall man and Ray collided. The man's papers ended up on the platform, and both men scrambled to gather them up before they got in the water. It was not until they parted that Ray realized he had just collided with John Wayne. He was getting into the liberty launch Ray had just used to go on his way to Ford Island to film some night scenes.

When he got home, he said to his wife, "Guess whom I ran into today?"

She asked, "Who?"

When he told her he physically ran into John Wayne, she became upset with his weird sense of humor. Ray couldn't imagine why.

After that tour of duty in Hawaii, it was time to return to the home port of Long Beach. Ray's good friend Rick was always so kind. He loved to help others constantly. He also was a born-again Christian from Arkansas. While Ray took the long slow trip back to

Long Beach on the ship, Rick volunteered to accompany Darlene and fly back to the mainland and even let her stay with him and his girlfriend at his mother's home in the mountains near San Francisco. When the ship pulled into port at Long Beach, Rick and Darlene were on the dock waiting. She already picked out an apartment in Long Beach.

You should know that Ray is one-eighth Cherokee. The Cherokee believe in one God they call *Creator*. When the missionaries explained about God's only Son, Jesus, most Cherokees decided to become Christian. Now, the Cherokee word for California literally means "the place where the crazy people live." Ray can see the logic in that. He could tell that most Californians were not true lovers of our heavenly Father, God Almighty. They seemed to be more interested in self. That is, they seemed to think of themselves. They believed in doing whatever they wanted to do. The crime rate was very high back then and still is today. Their representatives and senators are mostly Progressive Democrats with Nancy Pelosi leading the way. Ray saw them as being influenced by the dark world. They hate those who live in the light and criticize them constantly.

Jesus says it best in John 15:18–25. At the risk of repeating what was quoted in chapter 1, here is that scripture once again:

> If the world hates you, keep in mind that it hates me first. If you belonged to the world, it would love you as its own. As it is, you do not belong to the world, but I have chosen you out of the world. That is why the world hates you. Remember what I told you. A servant is not greater than his master. If they persecuted me, they will persecute you also. If they obeyed my teaching they will obey yours also. They will treat you this way because of my name, for they do not know the one who sent me. If I had not come and spoken to them, they would not be guilty of sin; but now they have no excuse for their sin.

Whoever hates me hates my Father as well. If I had not done among them the works no one else did, they would not be guilty of sin. As it is, they have seen and yet they have hated both me and my Father. But this is to fulfill what is written in their Law. They hated me without reason.

Now you can see why there is such hate for President Trump. President Trump is hated by the Progressive Democrats and is tormented greater than any other president since the beginning of our country. Why? Could it have something to do with his policy to hold a prayer meeting with various clergy every morning in the oval office before the day's work begins? Today, as an elderly ordained minister, Ray has joined in as a long-distance prayer partner with President Trump. He offers written prayers and suggestions. A few days ago, Ray received a personal letter of thanks from President Trump.

In the prayer gathering with representatives of various Christian denominations each morning, they pray for God to give the president guidance and help his policies so as to continue to allow this country to be blessed by the heavenly Father. Ray sees this as the battle between good and evil. President Trump is hated just like Jesus was hated by those who live in the dark world which is guided by Satan. They fight everything he does and stands for. It is a perfect example of scripture vs. culture.

The dark side wants to kill babies while in their mothers' wombs. They want to even kill them at or even shortly after the time of birth. The governors of both New York and Illinois recently signed a bill into law that babies can be terminated at the time of birth or shortly thereafter. That is simply murder. Those states that are passing laws that disallow abortions as soon as a heartbeat is detected are being stalled by the liberal judges appointed by Democratic presidents. Jesus said that those who live in the dark do not know where they are going. They want unborn babies and those at the time of birth to be killed.

The dark side wants to do away with our current constitution because, as stated by two Democratic senators, *It no longer meets the needs of our culture.* That means that every right under the constitution is no longer in effect just as what happened in Venezuela. There would be no freedom of speech, freedom of religion, and freedom to bear arms. Every amendment to our constitution from day one until now would be done away within an instant.

Back to the story of Ray's training by God to prepare him for his ultimate assignments, upon release from active duty, Ray had to find a civilian job. The main problem was that because of the "fake news" networks reporting of the Vietnam War, which was mostly made up by them, the people had turned against Vietnam veterans. They could only get a job at one place in the St. Louis area, McDonnell Aircraft.

Now there was one exception, however. Ray was invited to audition at a showboat near the arch at the St. Louis Riverfront. He was offered a job three nights a week for eighty dollars a night. That was a lot of money in 1966. Darlene did not like Ray being a musician. She did have one good point though. If the showboat decided to hire a different performer, Ray would have to look for another venue. The rest of her reasoning was that she did not like him performing music. With all his experience as a singer, songwriter, musician, and music teacher, he felt it was an excellent way to support the two of them. Once there were kids, the huge money would have been great. If he worked three nights a week at the showboat, he could also teach music at Ludwig Aeolian Studios at least two or three nights a week.

She won the argument, and Ray wanted to keep peace in the family. He went to work at McDonnell Aircraft who supplied jet fighter planes for the military and for allied countries as well. Many of the employees there were veterans.

Computers were something very new in the world. Only large corporations could afford the latest and very expensive computers. Ray heard about computers but knew nothing about them. But that was where the company hired him to begin work right away. He began to advance, but the pay was extremely low. He started out at $2.08 per hour. Upon his first real promotion, he worked next to a person who did the same job but was paid $11.00 an hour. That upset Ray. After working there one year, his boss was excited to offer him a $.25 an hour raise. He was insulted. Instead, he quit and went to work at a "sweat shop" where you were to operate several pieces of equipment including an IBM 1401 computer and at the same time physically run from one piece of equipment to another to keep them all running. Then he advanced to operate the newest IBM 360 computer.

He did not see this training as being training from God but simply training from higher-ranking humans. Looking back, he now realizes that this training would be very valuable to his ultimate career as a computer software developer. Ray began taking evening classes in computer programming and college courses in business administration. Although he was not the greatest student all through his school years, he began making almost all As.

On June 30, 1969, Darlene gave birth to their first child, a boy. Two years later, she had a miscarriage. But, a year and a half after that, on December 2, 1972, she had a baby girl. Ray had always loved children even when he was a child. He loved helping and teaching younger children. He loved teaching young six-year-old students at Ludwig Aeolian.

Ray worked his way up the corporate ladder quickly. He found that computer programming and systems analysis work was very similar to writing songs. The same skills were required in both occupations.

There was one drawback though. Due to an incident while on active duty in the Navy, Ray became disabled. Symptoms began to appear and multiply only months off active duty. It was a physical struggle to work and also attend college in the evening, but he made it. His last job was with a large corporation which had operations on every continent in the world. It was a $4.5-billion corporation. His final management position was as head of data processing for the largest division working on the staff of the division president. The political pressure was too great for his disabilities causing a decline in his health. He suffered his first heart attack.

By 1986, Ray decided to cash in all his executive stock in that corporation and founded his own computer company, RACOM Systems, Inc. It was a full corporation with stock certificates and corporate seal. Ray held the offices of president and CEO. Business was great; and he asked his wife, Darlene, to quit her job as a bookkeeper for a hospital and join the company as vice president upon becoming incorporated. She held the office of vice president. In a corporation, you must officially have four offices filled. Ray held the office as president and financial officer, while Darlene held the offices of vice president and secretary. They soon had a quickly growing staff of programmers, sales personnel, and a receptionist or secretary. At first, things were going great. Ray's parents bought stock in the company, and they had clients as far east as Louisville, Kentucky; as far west as Los Cruces, New Mexico; as far north as Chicago; and as far south as Branson, Missouri.

Then things went terribly wrong. There were health problems in the family besides Ray's own disabilities. Business was dropping off due to a poor economy in 1990. One day, Ray had a sales call way out in Grand Island, Nebraska. It turned out to be a "no, thank you." His company specialized in computers and software for small- to medium-size companies. With the declining economy, he could not get new clients. Existing clients did not want to spend the money to expand their computer software. The parent company had several subsidiaries. RACOM Business Systems developed software packages. RACOM Computers sold the company's own brand of desktop computers. RACOM Education specialized in training clients in word processing, spreadsheet software, and, of course, the RACOM software developed for them. Finally, there was RACOM Communications which set up small networks for larger clients.

Upon returning home from the failed meeting in Grand Island, Nebraska, Ray got as far as Kansas City and became too tired to continue further home to St. Peters, Missouri, which is exactly thirty-five miles from the St. Louis Riverfront. He was afraid he was too tired and could cause an accident and possibly hurt or kill someone on the highway.

Ray checked into a Holiday Inn in Kansas City to rest up for the night. He no sooner got settled in when he became deeply depressed due to the problems of family and the economy. He knelt next to the bed and began to pray, "Heavenly Father, You know all the things going wrong in my life. My father passed just a few years ago. My mother is in a nursing home following a fall and then a stroke. My wife had four failed surgeries this year. My son was mugged in San Diego causing permanent brain damage while on active duty in the Navy. My daughter is dating a boy who has a gun in his glove compartment and looks as though he has not bathed in years. On top of all that, I cannot get new clients for my company, and existing clients do not want to spend money to expand their computer equipment nor software due to the poor economy. Please, Lord, tell me what it is You want me to be, what is Your plan for me. In Jesus's name, Amen."

He waited for several minutes when suddenly the room became very bright; the light filled every inch of the hotel room but not from any particular source. Ray became deaf and could no longer hear the highway traffic outside. Then he received a telepathic message from God Almighty, *You are to enlighten others in an entertaining way.* That was not the message he was expecting, nor did he want that message. His wife still did not like him being a musician. She did not like the music he wrote. She quite simply did not like him being a musician, singer, or songwriter. She said she hated every song he ever wrote. That was the real reason she did not want him to take the job at the showboat at the St. Louis Riverfront.

Ray did not want to disobey God, but if he obeyed God, he was assured of being faced with a divorce. He had not been active in practicing music because of his wife. To please God, he gathered some inexpensive recording equipment and practiced by recording songs and self-producing cassette tapes. CDs were not yet invented in 1990.

Ray had moved his computer company in the spring of 1991 to Branson, Missouri. Ray had more business there in the first three weeks than what he had in the previous six months in the St. Louis area. One Branson millionaire started nine new companies and had

Ray develop all the software for each one of those new companies. Darlene stayed back in St. Peters to try to sell their four-bedroom, two-and-a-half-bath home. She sold the home in early 1992 and joined Ray in the Branson area.

Ray dissolved the corporation but developed one solely owned company that developed software and provided hardware. Ray developed new software for hotels, resorts, and even one Branson theater. Branson was becoming known as the entertainment capital of the world. There were more theater seats in Branson than in Las Vegas and Broadway combined. Many well-known personalities and celebrities built and opened one new theater after another. Instead of traveling all over the world, they had a permanent home in Branson and put on two shows per day—an afternoon matinee show and an evening show.

The previous problems with his family and company no longer mattered because God did not give him his first assignment until the year 2000. Ray practiced for ten years and produced some nice cassette albums including Christian songs. He only hoped it was good enough to please our Lord God. Then, in 2000 at around 1:00 or 2:00 a.m., he was awakened with a new melody running through his head over and over. He received another message from God, *Now go to your music room and jot down some music notation so as to not forget this melody in the morning.* Soon after, God directed him to a scripture in the Bible to use as the lyrics to the song he just gave him to write for Him.

This was repeated many times until Ray had enough new Christian songs to self-produce a CD of God's songs with even more songs left over that were not included in this first CD. Ray knew from reading 1 Corinthians that when one is given spiritual gifts upon being born again, they are not to gain financially from that gift. So he gave copies of the new CD to those who wanted one. Some people asked for a second copy to give to a friend who they felt needed a spiritual uplifting.

Ray's wife, Darlene, who suffered from severe rheumatoid arthritis got much worse. By the mid-1990s, Ray had to care for her while running the company. As time passed, she got worse until eventually he had to be her twenty-four-hours-a-day, seven-days-a-week caregiver. Ray bathed her, dressed her, colored her hair, styled her hair, and put her makeup on all the while doing the cooking, laundry, cleaning, and caring for the yard. Ultimately, he was told by several doctors that his own health was getting much worse. They said, "If you don't stop insisting on caring for your wife, you will not be around much longer."

A midnight fall caused severe damage to multiple parts of Darlene's body. She had to have multiple surgeries and ended up in a nursing home in which she would have to spend the rest of her life. Ray was not allowed to care for her because he was not qualified and not strong enough to handle her without additional help. Even in the nursing home, she had to be handled by two expert persons per doctor's orders.

While in the nursing home, their son, Mike, became ordained as an independent minister and began to preach to those who wanted a chaplain-type person to comfort them while in the nursing home. Then he was allowed to hold church services every other Sunday. He needed a music minister to play the piano for hymns. Ray, because of God's training, filled that position. By then, he had to quit work because his own health was too poor to be able to run a company or even work at any regular job. The Social Security doctor determined that Ray was not able to work for even two hours a day at a sedentary job.

Their son, Mike, sometimes had a hard time making the one-hour trip to the nursing home to preach; so his father began filling in for him as associate pastor. Ray knew he was already God ordained but realized if he was to continue to preach officially, he needed to become officially ordained as a pastor to satisfy the human population. In the next chapter about miracles, there is a miracle that took place while Ray and his son co-pastored at the nursing home.

Darlene passed on January 6, 2013, at 2:20 in the morning. The father and son pastors continued to preach, and the congregation grew quite a bit. They were well liked by the residents. Some attended the church services, while others preferred for Mike to preach and teach them in the privacy of their rooms. Then, suddenly, the activities director at the nursing home decided to fire them and have a secular entertainer perform popular music instead of holding church services.

Ray and his son both waited for a new assignment from God. After a while, Ray received a message from God one night in late 2016 while at home, *You did a good job writing my songs. You did a good job co-preaching with your son at the nursing home. Soon you will be given a new assignment. You are to preach at a place to which you will be directed.* Not long after that, Ray's daughter, Mary Ann, one of his sisters-in-law, and her husband along with a friend suggested he go into assisted living. Taking care of a 1500-square-foot home by himself while in a poor health condition was becoming too difficult.

Ray invited the administrator of an assisted living place near his home to visit with his daughter, Mary Ann, present. Somehow, the words just jumped out of Ray's mouth, "If I come to live in your assisted living place, would it be possible to hold church services there?" In seconds, the administrator responded with a definite "Yes!" Ray felt that this was the place to which he would be directed just as God had told him.

This new preaching job was so important that Ray contacted the fellowship which ordained his son. An applicant for ordination must answer many questions. A few were yes and no questions, but then the hard part was to give full written answers as to how he would preach about various subjects. These questions were to determine both if the applicant was already God ordained and if he was qualified. To answer these questions, one must have a working knowledge of the Bible. The answers to these questions were then given to the council of elders who would decide if the applicant was qualified to be ordained under the authority of Matthew 28:19–20. Upon completing the test, Ray was informed by email that it normally would take ten days to find out the results of the elders' examination of those written answers. Five days later, Ray signed onto the internet to check his email, and there was an email message from the fellowship waiting for him. "Your answers passed the scrutiny of the council of elders, and you are hereby an ordained independent minister." That is their term for what is commonly known as an ordained nondenominational preacher.

From the time Ray and Darlene first moved to southwest Missouri, God had directed them to attend and even join various churches of different denominations. Ray now knew that God wanted him to know about the similarities and differences of each of these denominations.

A nondenominational church was their favorite because everyone was very warm, and while the preacher explained his personal take on various scriptures, he left it up to the congregation to make up their own minds as to whether or not they agreed with him. They also liked the idea that there was no governing body that dictated what the preachers were to preach and what they were not to preach. There would be no arguments over minor disagreements. A nondenominational preacher simply preaches from the Bible and not from what a headquarters somewhere wants them to preach.

There was one very important thing Ray learned as the result of God's training. God's inspired words in the Bible do not necessarily mean one thing. While we humans write something or say something to others in order to get one single thought across, God is so much more intelligent than we mere humans that His words often have more than one meaning. In home Bible studies, Ray and Darlene learned that different people in attendance had slightly different views as to what passages in the Bible meant. Even when a person reads a passage one time and a month later reads the same passage, they often come away with a different meaning. Both meanings turn out to be correct. Therefore, when a denomination dictates that a passage in the Bible means just one thing, they are missing the whole picture. It is like the old saying "One cannot see the forest for the trees."

After being a resident for five months in the assisted living establishment, Ray realized he could no longer afford to live there. His monthly income would soon be surpassed by the increase in rent.

He prayed for God to tell him what to do. He asked God in prayer if he would be disobeying Him if he left assisted living and moved into a rented duplex nearby. God immediately gave His answer, *I told you that you had to preach there. I did not say you had to live there.*

At the assisted living place, the congregation grew rapidly, and a little over half of the residents were regular members. Ray knew that each sermon he prepared was God inspired. He could feel either God or Jesus or both over his left shoulder guiding every word. Ray would often write sentences that matched what God wanted to say in the sermon. But then, Ray was directed to backspace his writing and use different words that, to him, had the exact same meaning. God has a way of wanting only His inspired words to be used in the sermon. At the end of each service, Ray was often praised for his preaching. Each time he made sure the members knew that the words were those of God and that only God deserved the credit and glory for the sermon just given. The congregation would often stay around for as long as forty-five minutes after the service to discuss the sermon topic with Ray. Not just a few stuck around, but usually all of them stayed wanting to know more. Even in their old age, they wanted to learn. Some insisted on their new pastor praying a form of the sinner's prayer to be born again after listening to Ray's teaching of the gospel. Ray reminded them that while he was somewhat an evangelical preacher, he was no Billy Graham.

As time passed, so did some of the members of the congregation. Most were in their mid-80s and late '90s. They began passing away at a rate of one per month. Two were transferred to other facilities by their family members. Then there where those who became too ill to be able to attend church services. However, Ray was able to do God's work which he strongly believed was his primary reason for being assigned as their pastor at this particular place and time. Instead of following Satan's leadership of the dark world, they became born again and taken away from Satan. Satan did not like Ray preaching to them just as he did not like Ray and his son preaching at the nursing home. The residents included those who had not yet been born again, and Satan thought they were now his. Ray was able to preach with confidence from God that one can only enter heaven when they leave this world through God's only Son, Jesus.

Yes, Satan hated Ray for taking those whom he thought he had in his army away from him and having them turn to God. Eventually, it became obvious that Ray had done the work there that God intended for him to do. God wanted to give the residents of both the nursing home and the assisted living place one last chance to change and become true born-again Christians.

After hearing God's answer to whether or not Ray was supposed to live at the assisted living place, he moved into a duplex about a half mile from the assisted living place and about one-quarter mile from his previous home of twelve years. Soon afterward, there were only three members in the congregation. The last time Ray arrived to hold a church service, there was only one who just happened to be the son of a former preacher. He was already born again and knew the Bible very well.

Upon leaving his duties as pastor at the assisted living place, God gave Ray three new assignments at the same time. Firstly, he was to write Christian books beginning with this one so as to teach anyone who read his books what the truth was, what God wanted them to know. Just as Ray preached to his congregation about scripture vs. culture, this first book was to expose the readers to the truth about where our culture was headed.

You, the readers of this book, should know that these words are the inspired words of God. Each sentence was written as the result of God and/or Jesus's direction. You should also know that according to the Bible, when Jesus arose from the dead to rejoin His Father in heaven, he was given full domain over God's entire creation.

As was previously mentioned, God added two more assignments to Ray's authoring Christian books. The process of having a publishing company publish one's books is a very time-consuming task. Ray was to use the spare time to do two more things. His hobby of painting landscapes was to continue but with a new twist. God wanted him to continue painting, but from now on each painting must represent a passage in the Bible. Somehow the appropriate scripture must appear in the painting. Often it was best to put the scripture in a white cloud in the sky. The other assignment was to take the songs that were left over from the production of the first of God's CDs and have them on a new CD. This time, Ray had already written the music to additional songs given to him by God, but there were no lyrics from the scriptures. For the lyrics to these additional songs, Ray was to use his experience at writing sermons to research the Bible for just the right lyrics to go with each new song. That meant that the writing of sermons was also part of Ray's ultimate training to allow him to create lyrics from just the right scriptures for these songs.

When it came to the paintings, one painting is of a mountain and has the scripture where Jesus tells that if you tell a mountain to move from here to there, it will move. Another is of Jesus walking on water and telling Peter that he too could walk on water. The painting shows land in the distance with Jesus walking on water toward the boat with the disciples in it and Peter halfway between the boat and Jesus. The other disciples are in the boat watching. Another painting has to do with the scripture about soaring like on the wings of eagles. The painting is of an eagle soaring high in the sky. At the time of this writing, Ray completed a painting of Jesus sitting on a rock wall with children gathering around him. The scripture is where Jesus tells His disciples to let the little children come to Him. Then there is the painting, still in progress, with Jesus praying just before He was arrested and taken away to be turned over to the Romans.

To conclude chapter 2, I would like to explain that God placed the feeling in Ray's heart that all the training in music, performing before people, growing as a Christian, and the many experiences of learning about other cultures in foreign countries while in the Navy were all intended to prepare him to be able to preach about scripture vs. culture. The songs are intended to teach about scripture vs. culture. Quite possibly, someone or even many who now live in the dark world will see the light Ray is showing them as a result of that training. The songs, paintings, and books will continue to "enlighten others in an entertaining way."

Ray's publisher asked if he would be willing to be interviewed on television about this and the other four books he has written. At first, Ray did not want to be interviewed on television; but upon praying about it, God reminded Ray, *If you are interviewed, more people may buy the book. This does not have anything to do with the royalties but rather the number of people who could stand to learn the truth by reading these books.* After hearing from God, Ray informed the publisher that he would be willing to be interviewed.

CHAPTER 3

Miracles Executed by God

While we begin to examine the miracles in Ray's life, we will also follow the rest of his experiences in the form of assignments.

Concerning miracles performed by God to keep Ray alive, let's go back in time to when Ray was a boy and then all the other miracles throughout his life. Near the end, we will find out about one very miraculous miracle at the nursing home when Ray and his son preached together.

At age ten, the summer of 1954, Ray went on a two-week Boy Scouts campout. During this campout, Ray decided to take a walk. Now there is a rule in the Boy Scouts that one never goes off on their own. Just like in the military, there should always be adherence to the "buddy system." The buddy system requires there be at least two individuals when exploring or leaving the protection of the rest of the troop. Ray began to walk into the woods to explore forgetting to have another scout accompany him. After some time, Ray became totally lost. The woods were so thick that finding moss on the north side of trees was impossible. The sun was shining, but Ray could not tell from which direction. He did not have time to panic. He heard a message which he correctly assumed was from heaven, *Turn slowly and look for a very shiny light and follow it*. Ray turned slowly, and he could see a very shiny light but not like a light bulb. It was more like the reflection of the sun on a shiny metal object. He walked toward the light, and after some time, he was on the road looking at the side mirror of the troop's truck.

Not too long after that experience, Ray attended a scout patrol meeting held in the patrol leader's home. Following the meeting, the boys agreed to walk to the downtown area of their small town. Rather than taking the long way around by roads and sidewalks, they decided to walk along the top of a cliff which ran parallel with railroad tracks at the bottom of the cliff. The tracks were close to where the meeting was held and led directly to the downtown area where the passenger station was located. Ray was at the end of the procession and at one point got too close to the edge of the cliff. He did not panic thinking he could crawl out, so he did not yell out to the others. He did not think he was in trouble. However, the ground was loose and gave way. He slid partway down the cliff toward the train tracks below. Suddenly it felt like someone was holding him tight against the side of the cliff. A train passed below him. After the train had passed, whatever was holding him gradually eased up and allowed him to slowly slide down the side of the cliff to the bottom. He knew that about a quarter mile down the track and very close to the downtown section, the cliff ended and he could climb a slight hill back onto safe ground. There was no doubt in his mind that God had sent an angel to protect him. It is not too difficult to understand that God does this when He wants the person in trouble to be safe in order to let him accomplish His work.

What came to his mind was the passage in the Bible where Satan tried to get Jesus to jump off a cliff so that God would send His angles to save Him. Jesus told Satan, "It is written you are not to test God." Ray knew that he was not guilty of testing God because he did not ask for help; it simply appeared out of nowhere.

As a computer programmer or systems analyst, Ray was well liked by the management because he was able to solve program bug problems in record time. Ray decided at one point to not allow the coworkers and higher management to praise him instead of God. Ray could feel God giving him directions and often pointing Ray directly to the place where the program bug was located. So Ray told his coworkers that he truly believed that God was directing him. He knew that he was risking ridicule from the others, but it was most important to Ray that he cleared the air and gave credit where credit was due. Surprisingly, there was no ridicule—at least not openly. Every one of his coworkers believed in God. If anyone felt Ray was lying, they did not speak up.

While in the Far East, Ray's ship entered the Philippine Sea, and this was considered hazardous duty territory. The reason this area was considered hazardous was because the Chinese and all other communist nations recognized their country to expand to two hundred miles beyond its land.

This still is the accepted territorial border by all communist nations. North Korea used this boundary to, in their mind, allow them to capture any US ship that came inside that two hundred-mile limit. North Korea did capture a US naval ship inside the two hundred-mile area. China was a strong backer of the Vietcong during the Vietnam War. Therefore, it would not be unlikely that China or North Vietnam would capture any military ship of the United States or its allies that came inside that two-hundred-mile limit. Something did happen.

Before we continue with the event that took place that night requiring a miracle from God, it is best that anyone who is not familiar with the workings aboard a United States Navy ship be aware of something. Some sailors such as Ray have two jobs on board their ship. There is the job they do when in port. Then there is another job they perform while at sea.

Ray was a repair office yeoman (YN) on a repair ship. When in port, he and his coworkers handled the paperwork involved in repairing other ships. There is no way this job is needed while sailing the seven seas. It was the job of personnel with a job similar to Ray to stand watch. Ray's watch was on the bridge where the captain and other high-ranking officers directed the running of the ship. Ray would stand watch for four hours and then be off duty for twelve hours. This watch was manned twenty-four hours a day as they crossed the Pacific. The watch required the use of a phone which allowed for communications to and from the bridge with all other parts of the ship. The captain would issue orders to all parts of the ship, and Ray's job was to communicate those orders. Other parts of the ship such as the combat and engine room would either send messages to the bridge or request the captain's permission to perform certain tasks. Combat tracked the existence of any other ships or planes, and Ray would post this information on a Plexiglas board with a grease marker.

When there was not much going on during the night, Ray had access to a radar screen which was located at his watch station. This screen was designed for only one person to use at any given time. When the captain and other senior officers were not using the screen, Ray was permitted to keep watch on it as well.

While sailing within two hundred miles of Vietnam, it was possible that China or North Vietnam might capture Ray's ship. The ship was headed almost due north. While Ray watched the radar screen, he noticed that there was a ship approaching from the southwest and another from the southeast. Shortly thereafter, a third ship came into view directly ahead from the north. In seconds, all the ship's radar was jammed. Combat could not tell where these three ships were. The captain gave the orders to prepare to destroy all classified documents. That means they were preparing to possibly be captured. Tension was high on the bridge as you can imagine.

Ray believes that maybe, and only maybe, God stepped in and somehow put it in the hearts of the captains of the three ships to stop jamming radar and leave Ray's ship alone. Now please realize that this is only one possibility. It very well could have been that the three ships realized that this was a repair ship and not a fighting ship even though it was armed to defend itself. However, it was on its way to ports very close to Vietnam to repair the fighting ships that were in battle in the rivers of Vietnam. If this ship was captured, those ships needing repair would be out of commission and unable to fight. That would be an advantage to those who wanted to take over the country of Vietnam and make it a communist nation. The Department of Defense did acknowledge that Ray's ship did enter Vietnam waters.

Please know that it should not be assumed that God stepped in to protect Ray and any other member of the crew who was chosen by God. But, if there were multiple chosen people on board the ship that night, it would not be out of the realm of possibilities that God wanted to take action to protect those He needed in the future to do His work. One such person was the ship's Chaplain who was a Catholic Priest.

The captain did give orders to be prepared to destroy all classified material. This announcement was sent to all parts of the ship. Therefore, the captain must have believed these were not friendly ships. If the ship was given an escort through this hazardous area, the captain would have known that and not issued the order to be prepared to destroy all classified material.

After release from duty, life was almost quiet. Then three-and-a-half years later, their girl was born. Ray's wife, Darlene, became born again as her family was not all that religious. She attended church as a child by herself while the rest of her family did not. Ray and his wife made sure their two children attended church with them every Sunday unless there was an illness or other factors involved. Both children joined the youth choir and did study every Wednesday night at the church's youth center. Ray and Darlene wanted to be sure to raise both their son and daughter to be strong and true Christians.

One afternoon, Ray's whole family was in their vehicle returning home on a very dangerous road. It was narrow, and there was a place where the road had to cross over a high levee near a creek. On the other side of the levee, the road made a very sharp ninety-degree turn to the left. As their vehicle approached the levee, Ray saw a vision between him and the windshield. The Bible mentions the fact that at some point "young men will see visions." This was the thought that came into his mind. In the vision, he saw a man riding a bicycle just past the sharp ninety-degree turn. Alongside the man was a boy, possibly the man's son, riding his smaller bicycle just inside the driving lane where Ray would be driving in less than one minute. In the vision, the boy's bike slid in some loose gravel, and he fell to his left side blocking the driving lane. Ray turned on his four-way flashers to warn any vehicle behind him that there was something happening and it would be advisable to slow down. Ray told his family to please be real quiet and that something very serious was happening. Ray slowed to let the vehicle behind him get close. He crept slowly over the levee, and as soon as he rounded the sharp turn, there was the man on his bike and the boy next to him.

Then, just as was seen in the vision, the boy's bike slid in the loose gravel and he landed on his left side completely blocking Ray's driving lane. Ray stopped, and the man helped the boy up, and they both went onto the grassy area between the road and the creek.

Now this miracle of the vision was not to protect Ray. It was to protect that little boy, even though the boy probably did not know that God had a plan that required him to be alive and not be run over and killed. It is mentioned in this book because it was a miracle involving Ray and made a huge impression in Ray's mind that would stay there for the rest of his life.

At the end of May 1982, Ray and his wife took the kids out of school a few days early.

The plan was to see the World's Fair in Knoxville, Tennessee. They also planned to go to Florida to visit relatives and then go to Disney World. On the way home, they wanted to go to Elvis's birthplace in Mississippi and take the same road Elvis did to go to Memphis. They would then take the tour at Graceland as this was five years after Elvis's passing. The temperature at the World's Fair was over one hundred for the three days they would be there. On the third day, the family ate pizza, and then Ray's wife and both kids wanted to see something; but Ray did not feel very well and wanted to rest. The wife and kids went on, while Ray sat on a concrete wall to rest. Almost immediately, Ray started to bend forward with excruciating chest pains that ran down his left arm. He could see and hear the sirens of the electric golf cars that were converted into ambulances. Many people were having problems with the heat. Some might have been having a heart attack. Ray knew he was having a heart attack but was too weak to yell out or even lift his head and motion to passersby.

A few minutes before his family returned from their trek, Ray could feel himself regaining strength and was able to stand. Somehow the heart attack subsided, but he would find out later that some damage was done and some of his heart muscles died in that attack.

In October of 1982, Ray was barbecuing when Darlene stepped outside and saw that his face was gray. He did not feel ill, but she insisted he go to the hospital. To keep peace in the family, Ray agreed to go although he made it clear that they would find nothing wrong and send him home and they could not enjoy his barbecuing skills.

At the hospital, he was immediately admitted, and they asked if he had a cardiologist. The only cardiologist he could think of was his mother's. His mother's cardiologist arrived in less than an hour after being called. He looked at Ray's EKG and asked, "You suffered a heart attack within the last six months or so, didn't you?"

Ray did not want to lie and told the doctor what happened at the World's Fair. He then told the doctor that he felt he was okay and the family continued on to all those other places spending two full weeks on their vacation.

Ray was transferred by ambulance to a large St. Louis hospital with lights and siren where they were experimenting with a new procedure they called a cardiac catheterization. Today it is called an angiogram.

The only problem at the second hospital was that because the procedure was so new, Ray had to sign a paper stating that he was informed that he only had a 30 percent chance of surviving. The current result at that time was only one out of every three patients died. Ray was the third and last patient to undergo this new procedure that day. You are hereby spared the gory details of the procedure. When he was returned to his room, he could see both of the other patients who completed the procedure were eating dinner. He didn't have time to worry for very long. The crash cart was rushed to the room of patient number 2. Patient number 2 passed that day.

Darlene just happened to have the spiritual gift of compassion for those who were suffering. She quickly went to the other patient's room to comfort his wife who was grieving terribly. The hospital staff was not as compassionate. Thank God for Ray's wife who at least tried to help the grieving widow.

It should be noted here that the doctors noticed many blockages ranging from 20 percent to 60 percent. The accepted rule was that any kind of repair procedure would only be done for blockages of 90 percent or greater. They did inform Ray that his heart attack five months earlier did cause some heart muscle tissue to die. That was what the first cardiologist could tell from the EKG.

Ray, as president of his computer hardware and software company, joined several St. Louis area chambers of commerce. In the summer of 1988, he volunteered to help at one chamber's booth at a huge summer arts and craft show. Hundreds of booths featured craftsmen of either art or craft items for sale. There were many booths serving food and drinks as well. The chamber's booth offered free bottled water. The heat was near one hundred degrees. One of the chamber officers was also an RN for a cardiologist. She noticed some signs that told her something was wrong with Ray. She warned him about these signs knowing that he was a heart patient with a history of that heart attack just six years prior. She advised Ray and Darlene that he should see a cardiologist.

Ray told her that he did not have a cardiologist since the one his mother had passed a few years earlier. Both Ray and Darlene thought that since she thought very highly of her boss, this might be the best cardiologist for him. They made an appointment for a new angiogram.

On the phone with his new cardiologist, Ray was informed that they were able to get the information about the previous procedure six years earlier. The doctor stated that the two blockages that were 60 percent blocked then could very well be the cause of his current symptoms.

The procedure went without any complications. However, the doctor did find one blockage with 90 percent closure. While the access to the main artery in the groin area still was open and the instruments to reach the heart were already in place, the doctor performed a second procedure called an "angioplasty." This procedure calls for a probe to reach the blockage with a deflated balloon at the end. The balloon is then inflated at the location of the blockage pressing the blockage particles into the wall of the artery allowing for a 40 percent flow of blood to the heart muscles. It was also noticed that there were many other blockages. There were two at 60 percent, several at 50 percent, several at 40 percent and some additional minor blockages. This procedure in 1988 did not require any intervention by God.

Ray continued to see his new cardiologist regularly, and tests were performed to see if there was any change in his condition. It did seem that there were gradual differences even though his medication was taken as prescribed and he did his best to stay on a healthy heart diet as prescribed by the doctor.

In 1994, Ray and Darlene were now living in southwest Missouri, and he suddenly began experiencing heart attack symptoms once again. Ray's very close friend, Ron, since 1957 often visited Ray to help with Ray's company. When Darlene called Ron to let him know what was going on, he cancelled all of the next week's appointments and drove to be with Ray.

The doctor thought that because the symptoms were so strong, he probably had several of the larger blockages reaching the 90 percent limit. Even though it had not been confirmed that Ray was beginning to have a second heart attack, there still was a great possibility that this was what was happening. Therefore, this was not the proper time for Ray to demonstrate his God-given weird sense of humor, even though Ray could not help it.

Ron drove 225 miles to be with Ray. Now Ron was almost completely bald. When he walked through the door, he could see that Ray did not look very well. Ray decided to lighten up the atmosphere and said, "Ron, I really like what you did with your hair. You parted it much wider than usual."

His friend Ron could not help but turn his look of much concern to one of a huge smile and laughter.

Ron, Darlene, and Ray left for the hospital where an angiogram was scheduled. When they arrived at the admission desk, Ray handed the lady his insurance card, his driver's license, and a list of all medications he was taking.

The lady handed back the list of medications saying, "We will need this on the floor."

Ray immediately took the list and threw it down on the floor stomping on it saying, "Bad list, bad list, you stay down on the floor where you belong."

Darlene did not appreciate his choice of timing with his weird sense of humor. She said, "Stop it! They are going to send you home thinking nothing is wrong with you!"

All three went to the room to which Ray was assigned, but they had not put out a hospital gown for him to wear. Sitting in a chair, he became very ill and decided to take his shoes off and climb into bed without a hospital gown. As he lay there resting, Darlene and Ron talked.

Suddenly Ray felt a very warm feeling in his head. The warmth then traveled slowly down his entire body until it reached his toes. He then noticed that he felt much better. He said to his wife and friend, "Hey, you two! I just felt something come over me, and I feel completely healed. I feel like I could run around the hospital building three times without getting tired."

Wifie dear did not think that was at all funny. She said, "Oh no, you don't! You are not getting off that easily. You just stay in bed and go through with the procedure."

Soon after that, they came with the cart to take Ray down to the angiogram room. The doctor performed the procedure while Ray looked at his heart in the monitor. He watched as the probe went down each artery looking for any blockage.

The doctor said, "This is not medically possible. All the documented blockages could not have disappeared in one instance without causing either a stroke or heart attack. I am a believer, and someone else was with us today. You only have one 40 percent blockage where the angioplasty was performed in 1988."

Yes, that warm feeling that traveled down Ray's body was God healing him. There is no doubt about it. At dinner that night, Ray said grace and thanked God for healing him.

It is time now to enter the facts behind a miracle that happened while Ray and his son were preaching at the nursing home.

One Saturday night, his son called all excited because he received a message from God as to what the topic of tomorrow's sermon should be. He felt he knew the subject well and was excited about the next church service. Both the father and the son were familiar with Satan making one or both feel like they were coming down with the flu trying to keep them from preaching to the elderly. Many of those who were residents did not know about Jesus's command to be born again in order to get into heaven upon their passing here on earth.

They must have been considered to be in the pockets of Satan. Satan did not like anyone preaching Jesus to them. The next day, Sunday, Ray felt very ill as though he was catching the flu. He figured it was Satan causing this illness. He decided that since his son was so confident about the sermon, this Sunday he would just rest. After all, his own health was not the greatest because of his multiple disabilities. He sat in his recliner for only a few seconds when God sent a telepathic message, *Get ready and go to the nursing home. Mike needs you urgently.*

Ray knew he must obey God but took a few more seconds of rest when God repeated his message a little stronger, *Get ready and go to the nursing home. Mike needs you urgently!* He got up and got ready arriving at the nursing home fifteen minutes before ten when the service was to begin. He often would play hymns on the piano while the congregation would file in for the service. At exactly ten, his cell phone rang. It was his son, Mike.

His son said, "Dad, my wife is suffering a very severe life-threatening diabetic attack, and I can't leave her alone. Can you handle the service today?"

He agreed and began to offer the opening pastoral prayer. With his head bowed at the end of the prayer, he realized he was not prepared to give a sermon. Without lifting his head, he began to pray, "Dear Father in heaven, I…"

His prayer was abruptly interrupted by God sending the answer before he even asked.

God knew what his prayer was even before he could complete the prayer. God gave him the topic He wanted used for the sermon.

Upon getting home, Ray called his son to see how his wife was doing. Mike said she was better but not out of the woods quite yet. Then his son asked what topic Ray used for the sermon.

Ray told Mike, and his son replied, "That is exactly what God wanted me to use as the topic for today's sermon."

Although the next topic is not a true miracle, it is something that should be noted because it shows what it means to be a true born-again Christian. In the previous chapter, the story of Rick, one of Ray's best friends and shipmates, was mentioned. Now Rick was very kind and considerate as you read earlier. He helped Ray find the right apartment for Ray and Darlene.

When it was time to leave Hawaii, Rick paid his own way to fly back to California and accompanied Ray's wife on that flight. He took two weeks of his leave time to do this favor. He and Darlene stayed at Rick's mother's home in the mountains near San Francisco. Rick's girlfriend Carol also was staying with Rick's mother. When it was time for the ship to arrive in the home port of Long Beach, Rick, Carol, and Ray's wife drove to Long Beach to meet the ship as it came into port. Rick certainly did not have to spend all that money and use personal leave time to help his good friend Ray. But that was the way Rick was. He was a wonderful example of a true Christian.

Now comes the sad part which does involve true Christian compassion. Because Rick and Ray failed to exchange addresses when they left the ship in Japan, they were unable to contact each other. It was not until late 2003 that they found each other through the Internet. Rick was also involved with the event that caused Ray's multiple disabilities while on active duty. Rick's heart was failing. It was only pumping a mere 10 percent. He could only stay awake for fifteen minutes and then needed to return to bed.

Ray talked to Rick's wife, Roberta, for several hours. She told him what all had taken place since the two were together on that ship.

Rick married his girlfriend, and they had three sons. However, one Christmas day, she left Rick and her sons to run away with Rick's brother. Now Rick was forced to work and care for his three sons all by himself. He moved from California to Little Rock, Arkansas. That was where he met his new wife, Roberta. Roberta was not able to have children, and they both loved children very much. So they decided to adopt in order to add to their family. They did not just adopt one or two or even three children. They adopted sixteen kids. With Rick's original three, they now had nineteen kids in the family. All of them were in the Little Rock area to be with their father who was not expected to live much longer.

While on the phone, Ray got to talk very briefly with Rick for only fifteen minutes, and then Rick had to return to bed.

Roberta asked Ray to please write Rick's eulogy although Ray's health was also very poor and he was unable to attend a funeral in Little Rock. He sent the eulogy to Roberta who loved it.

Ray also decided to write a special song for his good friend. He named the new song "Rick's Song: You Are My Dear Friend." It took Ray forty tries to record because his voice kept breaking up at the powerful lyrics and of also knowing that his dear friend was dying. Here are the lyrics to that song:

We were friends so long ago, my dear friend. And then we were apart. Although we were apart my friend, you were in my heart. I wrote this song for you my friend because you're my dear friend. Now you must sail some troubled seas, and I can't be right there. You must always know deep in your soul, that you are in my prayers. I wrote this song for you my friend because you're my dear friend. We have sailed the seas together my friend, then apart over troubled tides. We will sail them all again, my friend. We'll sail them all with pride.

(Ray almost wrote that last line as "We will sail them all again, my friend, when we reach the other side." However, that was too close to mentioning his approaching death.)

I wrote this song for you my friend because you're my dear friend.
Now, we have reached the autumn friend, of our very fruitful
lives. And we do have a lot my friend. We can thank the Lord.
I wrote this song for you my friend because you're my dear friend.
Because you're my, my dear friend.
(Spoken) You are my dear friend, Rick. Love ya, buddy!

Note: For the meaning of fruitful lives, read John 15:1–17.

Roberta and their children bought a portable CD player. Rick listened to it over and over on his hospital bed and said it was his favorite song. He also insisted it be played at his funeral.

Roberta told Ray the doctor informed the family that the sense of hearing was the last to go.

Ray had to go to a VA hospital to have two stents placed in his heart. While in ICU, Darlene told Ray that Roberta called. She told Darlene that Rick was going to die very shortly but knowing that Ray was in ICU she did not know if Ray should be told. Darlene informed Roberta that Ray would probably be more upset if Rick was about to die and not be told.

On August 17, 2004, at 3:00 p.m., Ray was released from the VA hospital with his two stents working fine. His ride to take the 250-mile trip home arrived at 3:30 p.m. Ray found out later that at 3:15 p.m. that very same day Rick passed listening to his favorite song. Ray believes God gave him the strength to write and produce that CD so that Rick would know that he was loved by someone outside his immediate family.

Was this a miracle that they were able to get together at least by phone just before Rick passed? That is for the reader to decide.

This concludes this chapter on the miracles performed in Ray's life.

CHAPTER 4

Lessons Learning from a Lifelong Relationship with God

In this chapter, I will do away with the use of my name Ray. Instead, I will go into my preacher mode and explain what I have learned through my life experience and my training from God in order to do His work because His will shall be done. In the last chapter, I mentioned that God wanted me to return to my original assignment: *Enlighten others in an entertaining way.* There are many forms of entertainment: live plays, music, motion pictures, reading books, and others. The three forms of entertainment I have been given the gift to perform and trained are music, painting, and preaching. Therefore, in continuing to do God's work in my fourth assignment, I am producing Christian songs, painting pictures with scripture-based themes, and writing this book based on scriptures. These things are done in order to *enlighten others in an entertaining way.*

Who knows, some readers may like the bits of my weird humor I included in this book. After all, God gave me this weird sense of humor. I believe we are to use any and all gifts which come from God. Even though some readers may not like my form of humor, they will have to take that up with our heavenly Father.

The primary lesson I learned during all those years of being with God, experiencing all of the communications with God, the guidance from God, and the miracles God performed, is that one should not simply pray a form of the "sinner's prayer" and then believe he is born again for the rest of his life and need not grow or do anything.

In Galatians 5:22–23, we also learn more facts about growing as a Christian and bearing fruit, and I quote:

> But the fruit of the Spirit (within you) is love, joy, peace, forbearance, kindness, goodness, faithfulness, gentleness and self-control. Against such things there is no low.

This brings to my mind many persons who attended the same Baptist church my wife and I attended. One gentleman, during adult Sunday school, told how he ordered a new furnace and air-conditioning system. It came with a twenty-year warrantee. After the unit was installed, the installer asked to be paid. The man was proud to tell the class how he only gave the man half the money. He bragged how he told the man, "Here is the first half. Since it comes with a twenty-year guarantee, I will send you the second half when it does not break down during those twenty years." Now, readers, does that sound like a person who has grown as a Christian and bears much fruit which gives the person those attributes mentioned above in Galatians 5? In my mind, because I cannot judge, I do feel that this person should look at what he did and ask himself if he thinks he did as God would want him to do. The famous saying "What would Jesus do" fits this situation perfectly.

That same church offered a test to anyone interested in finding out what their spiritual gifts were that they received from the Holy Spirit upon being born again. Keep in mind that God expects us to use our spiritual gifts to serve Him by using those gifts to do His work. About 90 percent of those who took the test had no interest in using their gifts to serve God by doing work in the church. Imagine those who were gifted as teachers refusing to be a Sunday school teacher. A person with the spiritual gift of music refused to join the choir. They simply wanted to just live in the world and live with those who chose to live in the dark. That is the exact opposite of doing God's work and bearing much fruit.

Please understand that I am not judging anyone. The Bible teaches us that when we see a brother or sister straying from the way they should be acting, we should bring it to their attention. Some may listen, but some may be offended with someone trying to help them live more like Jesus.

Romans 8:5–10 teaches us about living in the flesh as in the dark world or in the Spirit on the side of God the Father. I now quote:

> Those who live according to the flesh have their minds set on what the flesh desires; but those who live in accordance with the Spirit have their minds set on what the Spirit desires. The mind governed by the flesh is death, but the mind governed by the spirit is life and peace. The mind governed by the flesh is hostile to God. It does not submit to God's law, nor can it do so. Those who are in the realm of the flesh cannot please God. You, however, are out in the realm of the flesh but are in the realm of the Spirit. If indeed the Spirit of God lives in you. And if anyone does not have the Spirit of Christ, they do not belong to Christ. But if Christ is in you, then even through your body is subject to death because of sin, the Spirit gives life because of righteousness.

Everyone should know from reading Exodus 20:1–17 that God gave Moses the Ten Commandments. These commandments are a fast-track lesson as to what we are not to do. The main problem I find with many people is they pick which of the commandments they want to obey and which ones they somehow feel are not that important and they can fail to obey them. We cannot pick and choose. One of God's original thirteen songs given to me is "Through God's Eyes." It serves as a lesson that we should not look at the world only through our eyes but we should see the world as God sees it. We should look at the world as though we are looking through God's eyes.

Yes, God gave us the Ten Commandments as a quick lesson as to what we must not do.

Each is as important, and none are to be overlooked. But God loves details, and in the book of Proverbs, He gives us lessons on how to avoid breaking the Ten Commandments. We learn in Proverbs whom to stay away from, whom we can trust, and the need to seek wisdom and keep it in our hearts—for God looks into the hearts of everyone, righteous and unrighteous. He looks for wisdom. Those with wisdom in their hearts also have knowledge.

One interesting part from a personal perspective is an instruction from God concerning my love of camping. I have a small travel trailer, and I wanted to go camping and enjoy the outdoors soaking in the beauty God has created. God spoke to me. He told me to go ahead and go camping and enjoy looking at His works but make it a working campout. That is, I was instructed to write sermons based on the lessons one can learn by reading the book of Proverbs. It was a series of sermons covering the chapters in this wonderful book of lessons. Because it teaches us many lessons of how we should live, it is, in my opinion, one of the most important books in the Bible. Here are the things we learn by reading and studying Proverbs:

1. About wisdom's rebuke. We should expect a rebuke from God.
2. Moral benefits of wisdom.
3. Wisdom bestows well-being and allows us to be healthier and live longer.
4. We should seek wisdom at any cost.
5. Warnings against adultery—how to avoid anything or anyone who would have us commit adultery.
6. Warnings against folly—again, what we should do and not do to avoid the hazards of folly.
7. Warnings against the adulterous woman.
8. Wisdom's call. This is a lesson on how wisdom calls out to us.
9. Invitations of wisdom and folly.
10. The section on the Proverbs of Solomon.

There are more lessons but too many to list in this book. There are thirty-one chapters in the book of Proverbs. The latter ones include the sayings of Agur and King Lemuel.

Here are things I learned during my life experience and association or relationship with our heavenly Father, and each is in response to one simple word:

1. Forgiveness: Scripture says very clearly that if we do not forgive those who have sinned against us, God will not forgive us of our sins.

    > For if you forgive other people when they sin against you, your heavenly Father will also forgive you. But if you do not forgive others their sins, your Father will not forgive your sins. (Matthew 6:14–15)

2. Love each other: Jesus issued several commands while He was God among us—"Emanuel." He commanded us to
    1. "Do unto others as you would have them do unto you."
    2. "Love your enemy as yourself."
    3. "Love your neighbor as yourself.

However, he eventually summed them all up into one final command, "Love each other," for we must remember that God is love—Jesus is love.

One final lesson from my personal experience with the Holy Trinity: God is forgiving if we repent in earnest. We must not do things in our relationship with God half-heartedly. We must do them with all our hearts, all our souls, and all our minds. God just may ignore us if we only do or say things without great sincerity.

Remember God is in charge. We were each created by Him, and He has the right to do things His way. We do not have the right to order Him to do things our way. So many try to make up the rules by which they will obey and expect God to accept their rules. In our earthly family settings, we see the same thing happening. The children try to dictate when they are to come home at night, what chores they are to do, and what manners they should adhere to. They simply reject the parental rules that "If you live under my roof, you will do as I say and obey my rules." So many young people run away from home because they do not want to obey their parents and end up being kidnapped, caught up in human trafficking, forced into a life of prostitution, or even physically and mentally abused and then murdered. Just as there are hazards when we choose to disobey our earthly parents, there are hazards when we disobey the rules of our heavenly Father. By reading the Bible, the best-selling book in the entire world, we learn about God's rules.

Here is the most important lesson for our youth as stated in the Holy Bible. Ephesians 6 states:

> Children obey your parents in the Lord, for this is right. "Honor your father and mother" which is the first commandment with a promise—"so that it may go well with you and that you may enjoy long life on the earth."

Please remember the combination of placing God above all things and then obeying His commands which also includes His Son Jesus's commands; by this, we can live a wonderful life. That is what God wants for every one of His human creations. He wants us to live a wonderful life to the fullest and in full abundance.

The biggest error concerning going under God's rule is the fact that so many people who think they are Christians say, "If God is truly a loving God, then when I die here on earth, He will give me a second chance when I reach heaven." Personally, I have no idea where that thinking originated. It certainly did not come from the Holy Bible, from God's words, from God's orders.

CHAPTER 5

Lessons I Earned as a Pastor about Scripture vs. Culture

Most of the lessons I learned as an ordained pastor were the result of God's guidance in the writing of sermons. When this is coupled with my lifelong attendance in Christian churches and Bible study sessions, there is a lot I have learned about scripture vs. culture. It can also be referred to as living in light vs. living in the dark. There is the evil world which tries its best to become the accepted culture of everyone on this planet. If you recall from the story about my life when I was given my third assignment as a preacher, it was God Who rebuked my feeling sorry for myself because I was living in an assisted living establishment. His instructions were that I quit feeling sorry for myself and use my time to study my Bible and be prepared to write sermons.

I realized that it was Satan who was making me feel sorry for myself. However, I am partly to blame for I did not put on the full armor of God as instructed in Ephesians 6:10–13:

> Finally, be strong in the Lord and His mighty power. Put on the full armor of God so that you may take a stand against the Devil's schemes.

It was Satan who insisted that I was not a real preacher. He was constantly telling me that even if I was permitted to preach, there would be nobody to preach to. He did not want me to preach about

Jesus to the elderly who were fellow residents in this place of assisted living. Then God stepped in and made me realize that it was His wish that not only I would preach but also He would provide guidance every step of the way in the writing of my sermons.

I have heard a lot of sermons in my lifetime, and with that expansive experience, I learned there are two types of preachers. One would write the weekly sermons from his own head. The other was the preacher who looked to God for guidance in writing his sermons.

My problem was having a battle going on in my head. At first, I did not realize it was Satan who was making me feel all those negative feelings. It was God Who stepped in and took control by His rebuke, which is actually a correction to my understanding. God made me realize that I was hearing from the evil side and failed to concentrate on what God had to say.

I am not alone in this situation. It is very true that there is a battle going on inside each of our heads. It is a battle in the heads of both the righteous and the unrighteous. This battle has been going on for thousands of years. Today we refer to this battle as scripture vs. culture. The culture of the dark world is the culture guided by Satan. The scriptures are God's inspired words. He chose and anointed those humans whom He wanted to use as the ones to write down His own inspired words which would become the Holy Bible. However, God's inspired words continue with the preaching of those who listen to God for guidance in preparing their God-inspired sermons. A sermon that is not God inspired is simply a bunch of words, and the congregation can tell that they may not understand what is being preached.

We were given a free will by God at the time of our creation. We hear the two sides in our heads and need to realize from where the two sides originate.

Make no mistake. There is a battle going on in your mind constantly. The battle is not really between you and other humans. At the risk of repeating myself, I will now quote from Ephesians 6:10–

12 which tells the whole story. Here is what Paul wrote to the church of the Ephesians:

> Finally be strong in the Lord and his mighty power. Put on the full armor of God so that you can take your stand against the devil's schemes. For our struggle is not against flesh and blood, but against the rulers, against the authorities, against the powers of this dark world and against the spiritual forces of evil in the heavenly realms.

It is the battle against the "spiritual forces of evil in the heavenly realms" which are Satan and/or his demonic beings (demons).

Satan loves to pretend he is God. When he puts ideas into your head and you think it is God speaking to you, you must know what to do to defend yourself against his evilness. My personally preferred armor to use against Satan is to put what you hear to the test. See which of two things I am feeling. If the little voice you hear or tele-pathically feel is good or about good things, it is probably of God, but don't be too quick to believe. I will explain later. If the voice is about bad things, it is of Satan—not just things about yourself but those of others as well.

Never get caught up in perpetuating rumors or lies. Rumors and lies are tools of Satan. You can hurt someone spiritually and even financially by repeating rumors. If you are not personally aware of the situation, do not get involved. It is of the darkness. Stay in the light. Shine your light so everyone can see, but never, ever, allow yourself to enter the world of darkness which is the world of Satan.

I remind you what Jesus says in John 8:44. Jesus is calling Satan a liar. He says:

> The father of lies and of all that is false.

What makes the growing culture around the world today so dangerous is that it is not new. It began thousands of years ago. It was present in Paul's day.

In Paul's second letter to the church of Corinth, he began talking about how some in their church tried to tell members of the church that Paul did not love them. He began in 2 Corinthians, chapter 11, calling such false apostles "deceitful" workmen, masquerading as apostles of Christ. Then in verses 14–15, he added:

> And no wonder, for Satan himself masquerades as an angel of light. It is not surprising then, if his servants masquerade as servants of righteousness. Their end will be what their actions deserve.

I can tell you from personal experience Satan lies to you and me. He loves to lie especially to good Christians, the righteous. He thinks he can destroy your desire to stick with God by telling you bad things about yourselves and about other people. Satan loves to do this gradually. He begins by acting nice and kind. Notice that this action is his masquerading as an angel of light and angel of righteousness. He will pretend to be God. Be very careful. When he starts off convincing you he is God speaking, look for flaws. Earlier I said, "If it is good or about good things, it is of God"; but in time I have learned that many good Christians, even pastors, are fooled by Satan's expert trickery. He is a very powerful foe. Before falling for his scheme, wait it out and look for a flaw. If something begins to look or sound different than previous words from God, then begin to take notice. Just like a parent knows the sound of their children's voices and children know the sound of their parent's voice, be aware of a difference in the sound of the voice or telepathic message you hear in your heart. If you suspect something is wrong, give Satan a little time to show his true self. As time passes, Satan will get a little more impatient and begin to make more mistakes. He will become angry and begin to sound "not nice"—not the sounds you are used to hearing from God.

When this happens, you know it is Satan and not God. He plants little lies and distrusts in small doses. He will see if it is working and gradually increase the dosage. He will tell you that you are no good. He may try to convince you that you do not deserve someone who loves you. He will try to get you to perpetuate rumors which is one of the most damaging things one can do. It is pure evil, but many righteous people fall for Satan's trickery and begin to do things such as perpetuating rumors which they should know is an evil thing to do.

For those of us who have an excellent long-term memory, he will remind us of all the bad things we have done—every little sin we have ever committed. Don't forget, if you are born again and you remain in Jesus and Jesus remains in you and you continue to follow Jesus's commandments, you have been pardoned. You are saved, and all sins have been washed clean by the blood of the Lamb and forgotten by God. If you let these lies persist and you may even begin to believe him, *stop*. Don't let this happen to you. Remember to put the feeling or voice to the test mentioned earlier. If good—God, if bad—Satan. Just don't make the mistake of trying to make the determination at the first sound. Remember it may start off looking or sounding good, but if it turns to the bad or dark side, you know God does not do business that way.

In Ephesians 6:10, Paul wrote:

> Finally, be strong in the Lord and in his mighty power. Put on the full armor of God so that you can take your stand against the devil's schemes. For our struggle is not against flesh and blood…

Some tell me that they rebuke Satan by saying, "In the name of Jesus, I order you to leave (or leave me alone)." I personally do not speak to Satan. I pray for God to help protect me. I ask God, in Jesus's name, to make Satan leave me alone. Note until I almost completed this book did I find a great way to test the spirit you hear.

1 John 4:2 states:

This is how you can recognize the Spirit of God: Every spirit that acknowledges that Jesus Christ has come in the flesh is from God, but every spirit that does not acknowledge Jesus is not from God. This is the spirit of the antichrist...

One day while sitting in my living room, I received a message I believed to be from God.

It was a message of rebuke. I was chastised severely about the songs I had written fifteen years earlier that were inspired by God.

If you remember when I was extremely depressed, I prayed for God to let me know what it was He wanted me to be. Then God said, *You are to enlighten others in an entertaining way.* I was both shocked and delighted that God had selected me to do work for Him. As I sat in my living room listening to this horrible rebuke about the songs I wrote fifteen years earlier, I began to put this message to the good or bad test. I realized it was not God but Satan. I should have realized if God ordered me to write and produce His songs and inspired their writing, then He would not have rebuked me for doing a bad job.

Don't think that Satan does not know you. He knows every little weakness in our beliefs and feelings. He studies us with very careful precision. If he can win us over, he simply strengthens his army which he plans to use against God.

So you must remember that the culture that battles scriptures is not only Satan but those whom Satan has won over to live in the dark world. The dark world is led by Satan. It believes in the things that Satan tries to get them to believe. He wants them to hate God and those who want to be in God and God in them.

Neither you nor I have the right to question God's wisdom or strategy. He knows what He is doing. He has His overall plan, both for the world and for each individual. His will shall be done, and God will prevail. To us, some things He does seem strange and not the way we would have chosen.

Take the "Battle of Jericho" for example. If you were a soldier fighting in a foreign land and your general ordered your company to march around the city for six days and then on the seventh day everyone should blow their horns and the walls of the city would crumble, you all would think your general was crazy. But that was exactly the order God gave Joshua in order to fight the Battle of Jericho.

Always remember the very old saying, "God works in mysterious ways." All we can do is put our total trust in Him. Just be prepared to do what the Bible instructs us to do. Put on your armor of God and protect yourselves against a very powerful adversary. The strongest armor is faith. Keep your faith in God. That is a very strong defense against Satan's trickery.

One time during my ministry as a nondenominational pastor, I received orders from who I thought was God, to write a new song for Him. I had much difficulty with writing the song. At first I thought it was because it had been over ten years since God gave me His last song. I was now older, and I thought my mind might be failing me. Maybe my song writing abilities were failing me. The whole thing began to seem very suspicious. It was so much different than the earlier songs God gave me. It was about things that were not of love and admiration. The way the voice treated me was completely different from before. Remember how I said earlier about how one recognizes voices of those close to them. That was how I felt. It did not sound like God. I even talked to another pastor on the phone about it. Before I got very far with this new song, I realized, "This cannot be God. This is Satan pretending to be God." I stopped writing the song, and God did not tell me I was wrong in stopping my writing. He said, *Your new assignment is to teach. You will still be "enlightening others in an entertaining way as I told you years ago."*

I don't know how many pastors have said to their congregations, "Sometimes even I question things." Yes, Satan is so powerful he can even begin to cause a pastor to question himself. That is powerful. I don't mean to scare you, but you need to be extra careful. Satan is a tricky one. He is a liar and a great pretender. Remember what Jesus said about Satan, "The father of lies and of all that is false."

Here is a second lesson about our battles with Satan and his dark and expanding culture. I am now going to address those of you, if any, who have not yet been "born again" as Jesus said to Nicodemus, being born again is the only way to enter heaven. He said, "It is harder for a rich man to enter heaven than for a camel to pass through the eye of a needle." Being good and kind does not help either for Jesus said, "Deeds alone will not get you into heaven." You must be born again.

Those of you who have not answered the call to be born again by praying a form of the "sinner's prayer," you must pray two things. That prayer, according to the book of John, states that you admit you are a sinner. Note: We all are. To say you do not sin is, in itself, a sin. Then you ask God for His forgiveness; you recognize with all your heart, all your soul, and all your mind that you accept Jesus as your personal Lord and Savior. John 3:16 says:

> For God so loved the world that He gave
> His only Son so that whosoever believes in Him
> shall not perish but have everlasting life.

If you feel like someone is telling you that you will be embarrassed if you go up in front of the congregation, that is the evil one talking. If something or someone makes you feel guilty and makes you not admit to God that you are a sinner, that is the evil one talking. These things are being told to you by Satan. He does not want you to be saved. He wants you to stay right where you are so he can win your soul for himself. Put on the armor of God. Strengthen your faith in God. Walk right up there boldly and be saved. Put Satan in his rightful place. In doing so, you will also put God in His rightful place. God is good, the light, the bright side, the loving side, the caring side. Satan is not good. He is of the dark, the dark side, as in the movie *Star Wars* with Darth Vader. Satan is not loving or caring. He is hateful and wants to fight God with his army. He wants you in his army and eventually fight God with him. He is the leader of the dark culture which is the exact opposite of what is in the God-inspired scriptures.

By the time you wake up and realize you have been duped, it will have been too late. Please know also that once you are born again, you must continue growing as a Christian. The Bible calls it "bearing fruit." Here is how you bear fruit. Read the Bible, obey Jesus's commands, and read the book of John 15:1–10; and you will soon understand what I am saying is the truth and nothing but the truth, because it is words inspired by God for John to write down for all to read and believe:

> I am the true vine, and my Father is the gardener. He cuts off every branch in me that bears no fruit, while every branch that does bear fruit he prunes so that it will be even more fruitful. You are already clean because of the word I have spoken to you. Remain in me, as I also remain in you. No branch can bear fruit by itself; it must remain in the vine (Jesus). Neither can you bear fruit unless you remain in me. I am the vine, you are the branches. If you remain in me and I in you, you will bear much fruit; apart from me you can do nothing. If you do not remain in me, you are like a branch that is thrown away and withers; such branches are picked up, thrown into the fire and burned. If you remain in me and my words remain in you, ask whatever you wish, and it will be done for you. This is my Father's glory, that you bear much fruit, showing yourselves to be my disciples. As the Father has loved me, so have I loved you. Now remain in my love. If you keep my commands, you will remain in my love, just as I have kept my Father's commands and remain in his love. (John 15:1–10)

The best part about being born again is twofold.

Firstly, you will begin to see things you missed before. You will see things that others still fail to see. You will be able to understand things that you did not even know existed before being born again. This does not all come at once. You will notice them gradually coming into your life.

Secondly, the Holy Spirit will give you one or more spiritual gifts. Read the book of 1 Corinthians, chapter 12. Paul did not list all the gifts in 1 Corinthians. I have no idea why. He even said in this letter, "There are more gifts, but these are just some of them." These gifts are superpowerful.

First Corinthians 12 concerns the spiritual gifts:

> Now about the gifts of the Spirit, brothers and sisters I do not want you to be uninformed. You know that when you were pagans, somehow or other you were influenced and led astray to mute idols. Therefore I want you to know that no one who is speaking by the Spirit of God says, "Jesus be cursed," and no one can say, "Jesus is Lord," except by the Holy Spirit.
>
> There are different kinds of gifts, but the same Spirit distributes them. There are different kinds of service, but the same Lord. There are different kinds of working, but in all of them and in everyone it is the same God at work.
>
> Now to each one the manifestation of the Spirit is given for the common good. To one there is given through the Spirit a message of wisdom, to another a message of knowledge by means of the same Spirit, to another faith by the same Spirit, to another gifts of healing by that one Spirit, to another miraculous powers, to another prophecy, to another distinguishing between spirits, to another speaking in different kinds of tongues, and to still another the interpretation

of tongues. All these are the work of one and the same Spirit, and he distributes them to each one just as he determines.

That is just a partial list, and Paul went on to mention when one is given spiritual gifts from the one Spirit, one must not use that spirit for personal gain or for fun. That is, if someone is telling the future and charging for their service, that is considered a sin.

Likewise, to use a spiritual gift for fun is also a sin, and the gift may be taken away. One must use what spirit(s) they are given to do God's work and nothing else.

God is, and will always be, the all-knowing, all-seeing Creator and the all-powerful God that He is. Be humble and do your best to spend at least fifteen minutes each day reading God's holy words. When God speaks, things happen. His will shall be done.

There is another important lesson I learned as a pastor about scripture vs. culture. It is the "fight against Gnosticism." What is Gnosticism? It is the practice of a false cult-type religion which tries to claim they "know everything," and although claiming to be Christians, they are the exact opposite. This is a perfect lesson in how a cult can become a popular culture. Notice the words cult and culture. They are related. A cult is the result of the dark and evil world developing the culture that people fall for thinking it is the true way of thinking.

The apostle John had a group of churches which originally followed his teaching.

However, this cult-type religion called Gnosticism sprang up from his early churches. In order to put a stop to their false teaching, he wrote a letter to the churches which became the book of 1 John in the Bible.

There are five main falsehoods which were taught by the Gnostics. However, some of what they taught are still the teachings of some who live in the world even today. Each of John's corrections about the five false Gnostic teachings is in italics for your convenience.

Concerning the problem with false teachers by the Gnostics to the churches founded by John, John began with an explanation as to what he was about to correct in their false teachings. John began by his opening comments in 1 John 2:26–27.

In 1 John 2:26–27, we read:

> I am writing these things to you about those who are trying to lead you astray. As for you, the anointing you received from him remains in you, and you do not need anyone to teach you. But his anointing teaches you about all things and as that anointing is real, not counterfeit—just as it has taught you, remain in him.

In 1 John 5:13–15, John addressed the Gnostic teaching of the lack of assurance of salvation. He wrote:

> I write these things to you who believe in the name of the Son of God so that you may know that you have eternal life. This is the confidence we have in approaching God: that if we ask anything according to his will, he hears us. And if we know that he hears us—whatever we ask—we know that we have what we asked of him.

About the total lack of morality by Gnostic teachers, John responded in 1 John 3:8–10:

> The one who does what is sinful is of the devil because the devil has been sinning from the Beginning. The reason the Son of God appeared was to destroy the devil's work. No one who is born of God will continue to sin, because God's seed remains in them; they cannot go on sinning, because they have been born of God. This is how

we know who the children of God are and who the children of the devil are: Anyone who does not do what is right is not God's child, nor is anyone who does not love their brother and sister.

The Gnostic teaching that Jesus was not the Son of God is addressed in five separate places in the Bible.
In 1 John 2:18–28, there is a warning against denying the Son of God:

Dear children, this is the last hour; and as you have heard that the antichrist is coming, even now many antichrists have come. This is how we know it is the last hour. They went out from us, but they did not really belong to us, For if they had belonged to us, they would have remained with us; but their going showed that none of them belonged to us. But you have an anointing from the Holy One, and all of you know the truth. I did not write to you because you do know it and because no lie comes from the truth. Who is the liar? It is whoever denies that Jesus is the Christ. Such a person is the antichrist—denying the Father and the Son. No one who denies the Son has the Father; whoever acknowledges the Son has the Father also. As for you, see that what you have heard from the beginning remains in you. If it does, you also will remain in the Son and in the Father. And this is what promised us—eternal life. I am writing these things to you about those who are trying to lead you astray. As for you, the anointing you received from him remains in you, and you do not need anyone to teach you. But as his anointing teaches you about all things and as the anointing is real, not counterfeit—just as it has taught you, remain in him.

Then in 1 John 3:23, he continued:

> And this is his command; to believe in the name of his Son, Jesus Christ, and to love one another as he commanded us. The one who keeps God's commands lives in him, and he in them. And this is how we know that he lives in us: We know it by the Spirit he gave us.

Also in 1 John 4:1–6, he continued his addressing right behind chapter 3, verse 23, above. This passage in which he continued his argument is known by biblical scholars as on denying the Incarnation:

> Dear friends, do not believe every spirit, but test the spirits to see whether they are from God, because many false prophets have gone out into the world. This is how you can recognize the Spirit of God: Every spirit that acknowledges that Jesus Christ has come in the flesh is from God, but every spirit that does not acknowledge Jesus is not from God. This is the spirit of the antichrist, which you have heard is coming and even now is already in the world.
>
> You, dear children, are from God and have overcome them. Because the one who is in you is greater than the one who is in the world. They are from the world and therefore speak from the viewpoint of the world, and the world listens to them. We are from God, and whoever knows God listens to us; but whoever is not from God does not listen to us. This is how we recognize the Spirit of truth and the spirit of falsehood.

John also addressed the subject of denying Jesus as the Son of God in 1 John 4:14:

> And we have seen and testify that the Father
> has sent his Son to be the Savior of the world.

Finally, in 1 John 5:1–5, John wrote the following which is known as faith in the incarnate Son of God:

> Everyone who believes that Jesus is the Christ is born of God, and everyone who loves the father loves his child as well. This is how we know that we love the children of God; by loving God and carrying out his commands. In fact, this is love for God: to keep his commands. And his commands are not burdensome, for everyone born of God overcomes the world. This is the victory that has overcome the world, even our faith. Who is it that overcomes the world? Only the one who believes that Jesus is the Son of God.

John also addressed in his letter the Gnostic teaching of disobedience of Christ's commands to love each other. He addressed this in five places as well.

In 1 John 1:5–10, John wrote about light and darkness and sin and forgiveness:

> This is the message we have heard from him and declare to you: God is light; in him there is no darkness at all. If we claim to have fellowship with him and yet walk in the darkness, we lie and do not live out the truth. But if we walk in the light, as he is in the light, we have fellowship with one another, and the blood of Jesus his Son, purifies us from all sin.

If we claim to be without sin, we deceive ourselves and the truth is not in us. If we confess our sins, he is faithful and just and will forgive us our sins and purify us from all unrighteousness. If we claim we have not sinned, we make him out to be a liar and his word is not in us.

In 1 John 2:29, John wrote:

If you know that he is righteous, you know that everyone who does what is right has been born of him.

In 1 John 3:10, John wrote:

This is how we know who the children of God are and who the children of the devil are: Anyone who does not do what is right is not God's child, nor is anyone who does not love their brother and sister.

In 1 John 3:21–24, John wrote:

Dear friends, if our hearts do not condemn us, we have confidence before God and receive from him anything we ask, because we keep his commands and do what pleases him. And this is his command: to believe in the name of his Son, Jesus Christ, and to love one another as he commanded us. The one who keeps God's commands lives in him, and he in them. And this is how we know that he lives in us: We know it by the Spirit he gave us.

Concerning the Gnostic belief in disobedience of Christ's commands, in 5:3–21, John wrote:

> In fact, this is love for God: to keep his commands. And his commands are not burdensome, for everyone born of God overcomes the world. This is the victory that has overcome the world, even our faith. Who is it that overcomes the world? Only the one who believes that Jesus is the Son of God.
>
> This is the one who came by water and blood—Jesus Christ. He did not come by water only, but by water and blood. And it is the Spirit who testifies, because the Spirit is the truth. For there are three that testify: the Spirit, the water and the blood; and the three are in agreement. We accept human testimony, but God's testimony is greater because it is the testimony of God, which he has given about his Son. Whoever believes in the Son of God accepts this testimony. Whoever does not believe God has made him out to be a liar, because they have not believed the testimony God has given about his Son. And this is the testimony: God has given us eternal life, and this life is in his Son. Whoever has the Son has life; whoever does not have the Son of God does not have life.

Then there is the fifth and final false teaching of the Gnostic—the teaching of not loving brothers and sisters in Christ. John addressed this in three places.

In 1 John 2:7–17, John began:

> Dear friends, I am not writing you a new command but an old one, which you have had

since the beginning. This old command is the message you have heard. Yet I am writing you a new command; its truth is seen in him and in you, because the darkness is passing and the true light is already shining.

Anyone who claims to be in the light but hates a brother or sister is still in the darkness. Anyone who loves their brother and sister lives in the light, and there is nothing in them to make them stumble. But anyone who hates a brother or sister is in the darkness and walks around in the darkness. They do not know where they are going, because the darkness has blinded them. (to my readers; that last sentence was first written by Jesus himself)

I am writing to you dear children, because your sins have been forgiven on account of his name. I am writing to you, fathers because you know him who is from the beginning. I am writing to you, young men because you have overcome the evil one. I write to you, dear children because you know the Father. I write to you, fathers, because you know him who is from the beginning. I write to you, young men because you are strong, and the word of God lives in you, and you have overcome the evil one.

(On Not Loving the World) Do not love the world or anything in the world. If anyone loves the world, love for the Father is not in them. For everything in the world the lust of the flesh, the lust of the eyes, and the pride of life—comes not from the Father but from the world. The world and its desires pass away but whoever does the will of God lives forever.

In 1 John 3:10–24, he continued:

> This is how we know who the children of God are and who the children of the devil are: Anyone who does not do what is right is not God's child, nor is anyone who does not love their brother and sister.
>
> (More on love and hatred) For this is the message you heard from the beginning: We should love one another. Do not be like Cain, who belonged to the evil one and murdered his brother. And why did he murder him? Because his own actions were evil and his brother's were righteous. Do not be surprised, my brothers and sisters, if the world hates you. We know that we have passed from death to life, because we love each other. Anyone who does not love remains in death. Anyone who hates a brother or sister is a murderer, and you know that no murderer has eternal life residing in him.
>
> This is how we know what love is: Jesus Christ laid down his life for us. And we ought to lay down our lives for our brothers and sisters. If anyone has material possessions and sees a brother or sister in need but has no pity on them, how can the love of God be in the person?

To my readers, that is a very powerful statement. How many of you still hate someone?

Are you guilty of not loving a brother or sister in Christ? If so, you, according to John, still live in the dark and are dead and no longer in God or Jesus. You fell in love with the world and followed the teachings of the world as headed by the evil one—Satan himself! I do not wish to offend anyone, but the words in the Bible are God inspired, so the writings of John in the book of 1 John are truly God inspired. Please heed the warnings John has written to his children, and if you are guilty of anything John warned against, you should repent and ask God to forgive you once again. I have learned that if one returns to God, God will welcome them back with open arms.

In 1 John 4:7–11, John wrote:

> Dear friends, let us love one another, for love comes from God. Everyone who loves has been born of God and knows God. Whoever does not love does not know God, because God is love. This is how God showed his love among us; He sent his one and only Son into the world that we might live through him. This is love: not that we loved God, but that he loved us and sent his Son as an atoning sacrifice for our sins. Dear friends, since God so loved us, we also ought to love one another.

My dear readers, you now have read the many words that prove that the dark evil world, which is full of antichrists and false prophets who want to guide you away from God. This false teaching by the Gnostics proves that they are the antichrists who live in the world even today.

The book of 1 John is a book that is completely a reprimand of the church to allow the teachings of Gnosticism to exist in them. It is completely evil. It is a horrible culture that if it were not for John, it could have spread quickly and become the culture of the world. Wait! There are those whose religion believes that Jesus was a prophet but denies that He is the Son of God. However, this religion does believe we should love our brothers and sisters and in the need for true morality, the obedience of Jesus's commands, and the loving of everyone. However, this same religion also has a subculture which believes by killing Christians, they will be allowed in heaven.

My dear readers, I know this has been a long reading of God's holy Word, but it is what is required in order for us to understand the lesson for the church people and teachers of Gnosticism. John was simply trying to turn the people in the churches he started away from Gnosticism, and he gave them the ammunition and power to be able to combat the teachings of this horrible and very evil teaching. You see, in order to address each of the false teachings of those who practice Gnosticism, we need to hear what John said in his letter known to us as the book of 1 John. Although this reading of 1 John was to teach us about how John wanted to combat the false teachings of Gnosticism, those same words help us to better understand ourselves as well. We do not advocate the teaching of Gnosticism, yet we find that sometimes we see ourselves falling into the same pit of misunderstanding as those who attended John's churches so many years ago. The words of God are as powerful today as they were back when John was attempting to eradicate false teaching in his church.

CHAPTER 6

Lessons Learned from Producing God's Songs

In chapter 2, you may recall the fact that God gave me songs to produce for Him. Near the end of chapter 2 was the story of how God guided me to return to continuing the writing of Christian songs. This time, the melodies did not come from God, but rather as the result of my Bible study as was used in preparing sermons. This, the final chapter, is not only the list of all songs thus far but the biblical support for the lyrics.

God's Songs on the CD: "Inspirations from God"

"Jesus Is My Best Friend": I was given a strong feeling of the fact that God's Son named Jesus Who could heal the sick, raise the dead, calm the sea, and perform many other miracles also just happens to be my very best friend. Additionally, the following scriptures agree with the reason one should have the strong feeling that Jesus is their best friend:

> You are my friends, because a servant does not know his master's business. Instead I have called you friends, for everything that I learned from my Father I have made known to you. (John 15:14 and 15; made known by the words in the Bible)

(This is a message from Jesus that John was to write for the church of Ephesus) Yet I hold this against you. You have forgotten the love you had at first. (Revelations 2:4)

Note: To love Jesus as your first love makes Him your first love above all. That is, He is your best friend.

"It's Our Quiet Time, Lord":

A time to tear and a time to mend, a time to be silent and a time to speak. (Ecclesiastes 3:7)

This was a strong feeling God was telling me about the mention in the Bible about going to a room and closing the door to pray in quiet. When you pray, you want to give our heavenly Father complete attention. In addition, since I am a born-again Christian, I know that I along with all who are born again will spend eternity with God in heaven. This song turns into a prayer thanking God for His only Son and finally for the time we just spent together during this quiet time of prayer.

"O Thank You, Lord": This is simply a song giving thanks to God for all that He does for us. There is a special thanks for the gift of God's only Son, Jesus, Who is the perfect Lamb—the Lamb of God—for it is quoted in John 3:16:

God so loved the world that He gave His only Son so that whosoever believes in Him (Jesus) shall not perish but have everlasting life.

"There Is but One God": This comes directly from the first couple of commandments of the Ten Commandments. God states (1) "There shall be no other gods before me" and (2) "You shall not make for yourself an image in the form of anything in heaven above or on the earth beneath or into the waters below. You shall not bow down to them or worship them for I, the Lord your God, am a jealous God, punishing the children for the sin of the parents to the third and fourth generation of those who hate me, but showing love to a thousand generations of those who love me and keep my commandments."

"We Shall Worship Him": In Joshua 24:15 in the last sentence, it states:

> But as for me and my household we will worship the Lord.

"Nobody Gets to Heaven 'cept through Him": In John 3:3, Jesus Himself states during His teaching of Nicodemus:

> Very truly I tell you, no one can see the kingdom of God unless they are born again.

In John 14:6, we hear Jesus say:

> I am the way and the truth and the life. No one comes to the Father except through me.

Therefore, the only way to enter heaven is through Jesus. The song says Jesus is the key, that is, the key to entering heaven. Then there is the very famous scripture of John 3:16 that states "God so loved the world that He gave His only Son so that whosoever believes in Him (Jesus) shall not perish but have everlasting life." You can't express this fact any better than this.

"Jesus Is the Vine": Quoting John 15:1–10:

> I am the true vine, and my Father is the gar-dener. He cuts off every branch in me that bears no fruit, while every branch that does bear fruit

he prunes so that it will be even more fruitful. You are already clean because of the word I have spoken to you. Remain in me, as I also remain in you. No branch can bear fruit by itself; it must remain in the vine (Jesus). Neither can you bear fruit unless you remain in me. I am the vine, you are the branches. If you remain in me and I in you, you will bear much fruit; apart from me you can do nothing. If you do not remain in me, you are like a branch that is thrown away and withers; such branches are picked up, thrown into the fire and burned. If you remain in me and my words remain in you, ask whatever you wish, and it will be done for you. This is to my Father's glory, that you bear much fruit, showing yourselves to be my disciples. As the Father has loved me, so have I loved you.

Now remain in my love. If you keep my commands, you will remain in my love, just as I have kept my Father's commands and remain in his love.

I received the deep feeling in my heart that one may lose their salvation. As an "ordained independent minister" or, in other words, nondenominational minister, I vowed not to get involved in disagreements among different denominational beliefs. This passage is very clearly worded by God, and God wanted me to include it in His song. I will not disobey God even if it means getting between interdenominational beliefs. Even though they are born again by confessing they are a sinner, asking God for His forgiveness, and believing Jesus is God's Son and accepting Jesus as their own personal Lord and Savior, John 15:1 states several very important statements by Jesus Himself:

My father is the gardener. He cuts off every branch (believers) in me (Jesus) that bears no fruit (does not grow as a Christian) while every branch that does bear fruit be prunes so that it will be even more fruitful.

In John 15:5–6, Jesus repeats Himself a little but adds the key thought:

> I am the vine; you are the branches. If you remain in me and I in you, you will bear much fruit; apart from me you can do nothing. (Now for the key thought) *If you do not remain in me, you are like a branch that is thrown away and withers; such branches are picked up, thrown into the fire and burned.*
>
> If you remain in me and my words remain in you, ask whatever you wish and it will be done for you. This is to my Father's glory, that you bear much fruit, showing yourselves to be my disciples. (John 15:7–8)
>
> If you keep my commands, you will remain in my love, just as I have kept my Father's commands and remain in His love. (John 15:10)

Since God directed me to this script for the song "Jesus Is the Vine," I had to obey God by including every word even if it went against the belief of some denominations that once saved you are always saved. One can determine that the ones being addressed as the branches are those who have been saved because they would not be in Jesus and Jesus in them if they were not first born again. Then, if they do not keep Jesus's commandments, they will no longer be saved; but "If you do not remain in me, you are like a branch that is thrown away and withers: such branches are picked up, thrown into the fire, and burned." These are the words of Jesus Himself, the Son of God the Father.

"The Bible Tells Me So": In John 14:1–3, we learn that there are many rooms in God's house and Jesus will prepare a place for you and will return to take you to be with Him:

> Do not let your hearts be troubled. You believe in God; believe also in me. My Father's house has many rooms; if that were not so, would I have told you that I am going there to prepare a place for you? And if I go and prepare a place for you, I will come back and take you to be with me that you also may be where I am.

The question now is: Will Jesus prepare a place in God's house for all people? The answer is *no*! Remember John 3:3 Jesus states:

> Very truly I tell you, no one can see the kingdom of God unless they are born again.

The only way to enter heaven is to be born again. All throughout the Bible, we find scriptures that infer that those who do not believe in Jesus will not have everlasting life: at least not in heaven. In this song, there is also the reference to the fact that Jesus is the only way for one to enter heaven. In John 14:6, Jesus says:

> I am the way and the truth and the life. No one comes to the Father except through me.

Therefore, the only way to enter heaven is through Jesus. Therefore, all these truths reflect the title "The Bible Tells Me So."

"Stand Up and Sing": It would require many pages of references to mention all the scriptures which talk about singing praises to our Lord God. Even the book of Psalms is actually a collection of songs. Singing is mentioned in thirty-two different scriptures; most are in

Psalms. Then songs being sung in praise of our Lord are mentioned seventeen times in different scriptures.

Here I will quote only two very important scriptures that totally match God's song "Stand Up and Sing":

> Worship the Lord with gladness; come before him with joyful songs. (Psalms 100:2)
> …Is anyone happy? Let them sing songs of praise. (James 5:13)

The most convincing scriptures are all throughout the Bible telling about the angels singing praise to God. If God was not happy with songs being sung to Him, He would surely not allow songs in heaven where he lives. He also would not have made my first assignment of doing His Word to be writing His songs.

"Children of Light":

> Believe in the light while you have the light, so that you may become children of light. (John 12:36)

Then in Ephesians 5:8–11, the words are used for the lyrics in this song:

> For you were once darkness, but now you are light in the Lord. Live as children of light (for the fruit of the light consists in all goodness, righteousness and truth) and find out what pleases the Lord. Have nothing to do with the fruitless deeds of darkness, but rather expose them.

We know also that those who are born again and will have everlasting life are God's children of light. They are to shine their wondrous light so that those who are still in the dark can see the ways of the Lord. One sermon given by a fine teacher said that when his family pulled their car out of the driveway every Sunday to go to church, the neighbors could see and quite possibly learn from them for they were children of light. Jesus said that those who live in the dark do not know where they are going. When some, who are in the dark, begin to look for the truth or a better way of life, they just may see children of light and learn from them. They may then have a desire to know more and ultimately become born-again Christians and children of light.

"Yes, I Believe": This song is one that simply confesses that whoever sings it believes in God the Father, in His only Son Jesus, and in the Holy Spirit. Additionally, he or she believes in all aspects of Christianity. To believe in them, then one must automatically believe in all of the scriptures which are God's inspired words. Now, a longer version can be found in a statement voice during many church services. It is not found in the Bible but is a statement or affirmation of faith known as the Apostles' Creed. This is the Christian church's statement in which if the apostles had a creed, it would declare all that a born-again Christian believes. The things that the Apostles' Creed states are also the things that this song states which a believer believes in.

The Apostles' Creed

"I believe in God the Father Almighty, maker of heaven and earth; and in Jesus Christ His only Son, our lord; who was conceived by the Holy Spirit born of the Virgin Mary, suffered under Pontius Pilate, was crucified, dead and buried; He descended into hades (hell); the third day He rose again from the dead; He ascended into heaven, and sitteth on the right hand of God, the Father Almighty; from thence He shall come to judge the quick and the dead. I believe in the Holy Spirit, the holy universal Christian church, the communion of saints, the forgiveness of sins, the resurrection of the body, and the life everlasting, Amen."

"Jesus Loves Me Just as I Am": This song is simply another song that states the same thing as the very famous and favorite hymn of most people, "Just as I Am." At the end of regular services, many Christian churches have an altar call. This is the time when those who want to be saved (born again) and be allowed to get into heaven go forward and pray with either the pastor or a layperson some form of the "sinner's prayer." Why play the song "Just as I Am" during that event? Simply because it is a song which states that Jesus loves us just as we are. We don't have to ask for His love. He loves everyone. However, in order to get into heaven, we must pray a sinner's prayer. There are many versions, but all of them include the three things that must be in the prayer in order for the person to be born again. Jesus said the only way into heaven is to be born again. One must 1) confess they are a sinner, 2) ask for God's forgiveness of all sins (past, present, and future), and 3) recognize Jesus as God's Son, believe in Jesus, and accept Him as their personal Lord and Savior. Stating this, the person becomes saved by being born again in the Spirit and, therefore, allowed into heaven. However, one must continue to grow as a Christian and "bear fruit" as specifically ordered by God the Gardener and obey or keep Jesus's commands. To be born again and then sit back thinking *All is done. I don't have to go to church, I don't have to read the Bible, and I don't have to do anything at all. I am saved, and that cannot be taken away from me no matter if I even kill someone, rob someone, hate others, curse like crazy, and live a life that is more like those who live in the dark world*, that is the culture that is popular and accepted by those in the dark world as being perfectly fine.

"Through God's Eyes": This is another deep thought that God placed in my heart. I was unable to find any direct quote in the Bible stating that we should try to see the world as though we are seeing through God's eyes. However, I once gave a sermon about this subject. God's message to me is that He is saddened that His children look at the world in any old way and ignore the fact that as the supreme "Creator of the universe," they refuse to look as though they are looking through His eyes. If they did, they would see the world the way God sees the world. That is the way things should be. The lyrics of this song state simply that we should "try to see the world as though we are looking through God's eyes." The best way to learn how God sees the world and what He wants each of us to know is to read what is written in His inspired words, a user's manual for all, the Holy Bible. Think of the Bible as a textbook written as inspired by God to teach all people.

"Jesus, We Praise Your Name": There are many passages in the Bible, too many to list here, that simply state that we are to praise Jesus's name. He is our Lord and Savior. He is the King of kings and Lord or lords. He is God's only Son and now sits in God's throne, with God, and God has given Jesus complete power over all the world. Upon being resurrected by God, Jesus was placed in charge by His Father. Therefore, we should worship God the Father, God the Son, and God the Holy Spirit. All three in one is called the Holy Trinity.

"How Did I Live without Him": Just like the song "I Saw the Light" written by Hank Williams and the hymn "Amazing Grace," it is a song that expresses how someone who is not saved finally sees the light and understands all the things that are required to be a Christian and to be allowed to enter heaven as one of God's children of light. Also, one should know that one must now do God's work and not simply sit back and do nothing. For the singer's life without accepting Jesus, life was not good. However, upon accepting Jesus and letting Him into his or her life, things begin to get better every day. Life with Jesus in it is noticeably better than life without Him. So one would naturally ask, "How did I live without him?"

CHAPTER 7

New Songs Written as though They Were a Sermon

In chapter 2, the story of how God guided my life to eventually do His work ended with my final assignment. I was to once again "enlighten others in an entertaining way." God wanted me to add more songs to the original CD he had me write. These additional songs, however, would be once written from the Bible with lyrics that could be in a sermon I would write with guidance from God. There are also others songs that I felt God would like to have included in order to make this a CD people would love to listen to over and over, not because I am a great songwriter but because these are songs that God has inspired in one way or another. Some songs are mine, and some are from other songwriters.

"The One I Love": This song was written by me as a popular music love song. One night, God gave me the message, *Who is the one you love the most and is your best friend?* In the book of Revelations, Jesus held one thing against the church of Ephesus in Revelation 2:4:

> Yet I hold this against you: You have forsaken the love you had at first.

When I heard this from God, I knew that the love song must not be about a woman but a song about the main one I love, Jesus. I threw away the original lyrics and rewrote them to show that the one I love is Jesus!

"Just as I Am": This, of course, is not my song but rather a very famous hymn that, as mentioned earlier, is often played quietly at what is called the "altar call." It is played while those who decide to come forward pray a form of the sinner's prayer and become born again. However, because I am one-eighth Cherokee and the author of the *Little Bear Cherokee Language Course*, I translated this famous song into the Cherokee language. Believe it or not, I sing this song in the Cherokee language.

"The Second Coming": The Cherokee chiefs, when told about Jesus by the European missionaries, knew that this made sense. You see, the Cherokee believe in one God Whom they call Creator (*oo nay lah nuh hee*) because they believe as Christians do that God created the entire universe. They so loved the melody of the song "Amazing Grace" that they wrote their own lyrics about the second coming of Jesus. Again, I sing this song in the Cherokee language.

"Rebuke: Correction or Condemnation": This song was written as though it was a sermon teaching that God rebukes those He loves as any father rebukes his children because he loves them. If he did not love them, he would let them get into trouble and do as they please without any guidance from him. God gives guidance to His children whom He loves deeply by rebuking them when they do wrong. It is written that when God rebukes His children, they should not let that harden their hearts. It is for their own protection and good that they receive correction from God in the form of a rebuke. Now as for those who are not included as His children or the children of light, God's rebuke is condemnation. In Romans 3:8, it is written:

> Why not say—as some slanderously claim
> that we say—"let us do evil and good may result"?

Their condemnation is just! I would like to remind you now that the book of Proverbs is God's inspired Word and is kind of a manual as to how to avoid doing wrong, especially doing wrong according to the Ten Commandments:

> How I hated discipline! How my heart spumed corrections! (Proverbs 5:12)
> For this command is a lamp, this teaching is a light, and correction and instruction are the way to life. (Proverbs 6:23)
> Whoever heeds discipline shows the way to life, but whoever ignores correction leads others astray. (Proverbs 10:17)
> Whoever loves discipline loves knowledge, but whoever hates correction is stupid. (Proverbs 12:1)
> Whoever disregards discipline comes to poverty and shame, but whoever heed correction is honored. (Proverbs 13:18)

And finally, in Proverbs 15:5–32, there is much more said about correction. It is much too long to include in this explanation about this song.

"Oh Jesus, You Are in My Life": During the first six years of the twenty-first century, God gave me the songs that were included in the original CD containing only fifteen songs. However, God gave me additional songs that were not recorded or placed on that original CD. I found the additional songs and am in the progress of including them in the second edition of His CD. These are both the songs left off the original CD and the ones that were written as though they were from a sermon. This particular song tells about the joy that exists when Jesus is in one's life. The biblical quotes would include the prayer Jesus prayed just before His arrest when He prayed for those who are God's children—the born-again Christians:

My prayer is not for them alone (referring to his disciples). I pray also for those who will believe in me through their message, that all of them may be one, Father, just as you are in me and I am in you.

May they also be in us so that the world may believe that you have sent me. I have given them the glory that you gave me, that they may be one as we are one—In them and you in me—so that they may be brought to complete unity. Then the world will know that you sent me and have loved them even as you have loved me. Father, I want those you have given me to be with me where I am and to see my glory, the glory you have given me because you loved me before the creation of the world. Righteous Father, though the world does not know you, I know you, and they know that you have sent me. I have made you known to them, and will continue to make you known in order that the love you have for me may be in them and that I myself may be in them. (John 17:20–26)

"Only He Can Set You Free": It is a different set of lyrics but with the same lesson as "Nobody Gets to Heaven 'cept through Him":

I am the way and the truth and the life.
No one comes to the Father except through me.
(John 14:6)

Only through Jesus can you be set free from your sins because Jesus paid the price for your sins by suffering and dying on the cross as the Lamb of God.

"A Sinner's Prayer": This song is simply one version of what the "sinner's prayer" should contain. First, you confess you are a sinner, then you ask for God's forgiveness, and finally you accept Jesus as God's only Son and as your personal Lord and Savior. Firstly, let us quote some passages that demand that we must repent in order for God to forgive us our sins. In the Lord's Prayer, we read "Forgive us our debts (sins) as we forgive our debtors (those who have sinned against us)." When Jesus first began to preach, He said in Matthew 4:17:

> Repent, for the kingdom of heaven has come near.

In Luke 13:3, Jesus says:

> I tell you, no! but unless you repent, you too will all perish.

Luke 17:3 states:

> So watch yourselves. If your brother or sister sins against you rebuke them; and if they repent forgive them.

Secondly, we must accept the fact that Jesus is God's only Son. In John 3:16, we find that accepting Jesus is a must in order to get into heaven:

> For God so loved the world that He gave His only Son so that whosoever believes in Him shall not perish but have everlasting life.

In so doing, we not only believe that Jesus is God's only Son but that He was sent by God to allow a way for us to be accepted into heaven. Therefore, if we accept Jesus as our personal Lord and Savior, we are asking Jesus to be in us and we in Him just as was in Jesus's prayer before He was arrested. He asked God to allow those God has given Him to be in us (Jesus and God) and we in them.

In John 17, Jesus says:

> Father, just as you are in me and I am in you. May they also be in us so that the world may believe that you have sent me. I have given them the glory that you gave me, that they may be one as we are one—In them and you in me—so that they may be brought to complete unity.

So, if being born again allows for the forgiveness of our sins by God and as we believe in Jesus as God's only Son and we also accept Him as our personal Lord and Savior, we are asking God to allow us to be saved, give us salvation, and allow us into heaven. Before being born again, we are unclean, and nothing that is unclean is allowed in heaven. Upon being born again, we are now clean and therefore allowed in heaven.

"Yes, God Loves His Children": Rather than rewriting all the entries which have been mentioned earlier, we know that God calls those whom He considers His children, His children of light. These are the ones who are born again; and God, Jesus, and the Holy Spirit are in them and they are in the Holy Trinity as well. Jesus prayed for that in John 17, once again:

> Father, just as you are in me and I am in you. May they also be in us so that the world may believe that you have sent me. I have given them the glory that you gave me, that they may be one as we are one—In them and you in me—so that they may be brought to complete unity.

"Jesus, You Are My First Love": This is a different angle about Jesus being one's first love. As quoted earlier, Jesus held one thing against the church of Ephesus in Revelation 2:4:

> Yet I hold this against you: You have forsaken the love you had at first.

"Before You Say, Be Sure to Pray": The Bible teaches us that we should be long on ears and short on mouth. In James 1:19, we read:

> My dear brothers and sisters, take note of this: Everyone should be quick to listen, slow to speak and slow to become angry, because human anger does not produce the righteousness that God desires.

Therefore, get rid of all moral filth and the evil that is so prevalent and humbly accept the Word planted in you, which can save you.

Do not merely listen to the Word, and so deceive yourselves. Do what it says. Anyone who listens to the Word but does not do what it says is like someone who looks at his face in a mirror and, after looking at himself, goes away and immediately forgets what he looks like. But whoever looks intently into the perfect law that gives freedom and continues in it not forgetting what they have heard, but doing it, they will be blessed in what they do.

Those who consider themselves religious and yet do not keep a tight rein on their tongues deceive themselves, and their religion is worthless. Religion that God our Father accepts as pure and faultless is this: "to look after orphans and widows in their distress and to keep oneself from being polluted by the world."

My personal feeling is that when we speak, it is best to ask ourselves, "What would Jesus want me to say?" Therefore, if we begin to say something that may hurt another's feelings or bring up a subject that is very controversial, we may be wise to pray about it first and find out if we should even bring up the subject we were about to talk about. So, before you say something, pray about it first.

Besides being a lesson from the words just taken from the Bible, it is also simply common sense. Those who read the Bible and know what God the Father and God the Son want us to say, yet speak as they want without careful thought first, are deceiving themselves. Now, to quote Forrest from *Forrest Gump*, "And that's all I have to say about that."

"Make Your Father Proud": There is little about the topic of making your Father (God) proud of you in the Bible. However, common sense tells us that if we do the things God expects us to do and Jesus taught us to do, we hopefully will make God proud. We want to please Him. In the "Children of Light" song, we learned from the scripture quoted that we are to "find out what pleases Him." If we try to find out what pleases Him, we are actually searching for the things that would make God proud of us.

"Only He!": This is simply another melody with another set of lyrics which say the same thing as some of the other songs about Jesus being the only way to heaven. Again I quote John 14:6:

> I am the way and the truth and the life. No
> one comes to the Father except through me.

"We Praise You with Our Songs": There is much about songs sung joyfully throughout the Bible. In Ephesians 5, we learn again about the darkness of the world's culture vs. the teachings of the scriptures and the fact that songs are even included. Let us begin by quoting Ephesians 5:8–20:

> For you were once darkness, but now you
> are light in the Lord. Live as children of light for
> the fruit of the light consists in all goodness, righ-
> teousness and truth and find out what pleases the

Lord. It is shameful even in mention what the disobedient do in secret. But everything exposed by the light becomes visible—and everything that is illuminated becomes a light. His is why it is said: "Wake up, sleeper, rise from the dead, and Christ will shine on you."

Be careful, then, how you live—not as unwise but as wise, making the most of every opportunity, because the days are evil. Therefore do not be foolish, but understand what the Lord's will is. Do not get drunk on wine, which leads to debauchery. Instead, be filled with the Spirit, speaking to one another with psalms, hymns, and songs from the Spirit. Sing and make music from your heart to the Lord, always giving thanks to God the Father for everything, in the name of Our Lord Jesus Christ.

"Looking for Direction in Your Life": This was the subject of a sermon I once wrote. In Psalms, we find much is said about direction. The ultimate lesson is that we should look for direction from within ourselves. Why? Because those who are born again have the Holy Trinity in them and they are in the Holy Trinity as Jesus prayed just before He was arrested. However, in Psalms, we find that God's inspired words there teach us valuable lessons on finding direction in our lives:

> By day the Lord directs his love, at night his song is with me—a prayer to the God of my life. (Psalms 42:8)
> Direct me in the path of your commands, for there I find delight. (Psalms 119:35)
> Direct my footsteps according to your word; let no sin rule over me. (Psalms 119:133)

Please remember about the book of Proverbs. It is God's detailed direction as to how to avoid doing evil or falling for schemes from those who do evil. Again, it is the dark world or culture against the scriptures:

> A person's steps are directed by the Lord. How then can anyone understand their own way? (Proverbs 20:24)

The lesson here is that direction should be from the Lord and not from your own way. In Jeramiah 10:23, we find Jeramiah's prayer:

> Lord, I know that people's lives are not their own; it is not for them to direct their steps.

Also Jeramiah chapter 13 describes a series of directions from God, and Jeramiah did exactly as God asked each time immediately and without question:

> This is what the Lord said to me: "Go and buy a linen belt and put it around your waist, but do not let it touch water." So, I bought a belt, as the Lord directed, and put it around my waist. Then the word of the Lord came to me a second time: "Take the belt you bought and are wearing around your waist and go now to Perath and hide it there in a crevice in the rocks." So, I went and hid it at Perath, as the Lord told me. Many days later the Lord said to me, "Go now to Perath and get the belt I told you to hide there." So, I went to Perath and dug up the belt and took it from the place where I had hidden it, but now it was ruined and completely useless. Then the word of the Lord came to me: This is what the Lord says: "In the same way I will ruin the pride

of Judah and the great pride of Jerusalem. These wicked people, who refuse to listen to my words, who follow the stubbornness of their hearts and go after other gods to serve and worship them, will be like this belt—completely useless! For as a belt is bound around the waist, so I bound all the people of Israel and all the people of Judah to me," declares the Lord. "To be my people for my renown and praise and honor. But they have not listened."

Just as Jeramiah followed the Lord God's directions, we find the same degree of obedience to God in the story of Noah who built the ark. Even when the people who lived near Noah laughed at him and mocked him, he did not waver. He built the ark to the exact specifications of which God directed him:

> So Eleazar the priest collected the bronze censers brought by those who had been burned to death, and he had them hammered out to overlay the altar, as the Lord directed him through Moses. (Numbers 16:39–40)

In Isaiah 48:17, Isaiah was a prophet, and this is what he prophesied:

> This is what the Lord says—your Redeemer, the Holy One of Israel: "I am the Lord your God, who teaches you what is best for you, who directs you in the way you should go."

Well, in conclusion, I would like to thank readers of this book for their patience and understanding. The only purpose in writing this book is to preach in an entertaining way which is my job assigned to me by our heavenly Father. We have a wonderful, gracious, loving

God Who shows His love for His children, those who are born again every day. If you learned just one thing from this book, it is to stay away from the dark culture that will try its best to lead you astray and away from God. Those of the dark world not only do not know where they are going, according to Jesus; but they hate those who are righteous, good, loving, caring, and compassionate. God loves those who strive to be righteous, but He looks into the hearts of everyone, righteous and unrighteous. He knows what we are made of, and there is no way to fool Him. We need to remember that God is in control and we must obey His rules. By living on this earth, we are living under His roof, so to speak. That means we must obey His demands and wishes and we must try our best to do the things and live a life that pleases Him. We must look within ourselves for direction in our lives. We must put the Holy Trinity first and above all things of this earth. Now, do not take exception when I say that this means we must put God before our families. Remember the story in the Bible when Abraham was tested by God when God ordered him to sacrifice his only son Isaac. If God inspired that story to be included in His book, the Holy Bible, then He must have meant every word. He, God, must come first. From the Ten Commandments to the wishes of Jesus that we be in them and they be in us, this tells us that they must remain in the number one spot in our daily lives. Many people, including me, talk to God often; and even though it is considered prayer, it is not always in a formal prayer setting. We must look to God in all that we do.

These are the lessons of this book. If you read it and come away with that understanding, then I feel I have pleased God with this, my fourth assignment in doing God's work.

I did exactly as a preacher is expected to do. I preached directly from the Bible and did not include any thoughts and lessons taught by those who live in the dark culture. Rather, I tried my best to teach all readers the lessons to be learned by reading the Bible. That is why I tried to quote those scriptures which are concerned with the topic of each song and the history of my life under God's guidance and teaching.

CHAPTER 8

The Need for Disciples

God does not complete giving assignments to those He wants to be His disciples. You see, God wants as many of His children to be His disciples. That is, God wants us to be pruned to the point where we are true disciples of Christ. What constitutes a disciple? A disciple is one who follows God's and/or Jesus's direction to teach those who are living in the dark world the truth as found in the four gospels, Matthew, Mark, Luke, and John. Additionally, they must teach those who grow as Christians and are no longer in the dark world the lessons that can be learned by knowing what is taught in the letters written by the early disciples

Firstly, there are those letters written to the early Christian churches. These letters became the books of the Bible: Romans, 1 and 2 Corinthians, Galatians, Ephesians, Philippians, Colossians, 1 and 2 Thessalonians, Philemon, Hebrews, James, 1 and 2 Peter, 1 and 2 and 3 John, and finally Jude.

Secondly, there are the letters written to those who were to be leaders in the early churches. These include 1 and 2 Timothy and Titus. Paul made Timothy the first elder or deacon, and Titus was Paul's very close friend.

God, as I said earlier, prunes those who bear fruit so that they may become even more fruitful. In the passages found in John chapter 15, the term fruitful means that they grow as a Christian. Once one becomes a true Christian by being born again, there are assignments issued by the Father to make them grow as a Christian. Yes, He prunes the fruitful ones so that they are able to do even more work for Him.

I thought I had completed God's book which He ordered me to write. I was wrong in assuming that. God is never done with issuing assignments to those He anoints to do His work. What is God's work? To teach others, enlighten others about the truth, the good news, and the lessons to be learned in the letters of the early disciples.

I now realize God wanted me to write His song "Jesus Is the Vine" not only to educate me but to educate those to whom I will be acting as a disciple, a teacher, and ultimately an ordained preacher. God was causing me to grow. I was being pruned so as to be able to do even more of God's assigned work. Let's reread John 15 to clarify what I just wrote.

John 15:1–4 contains several very important statements by Jesus Himself:

> I am the true vine, and my father is the gardener.
>
> He cuts off every branch (believers) in me (Jesus) that bears no fruit (does not grow as a Christian) while every branch that does bear fruit he prunes so that it will be even more fruitful.
>
> You are already clean because of the word I have spoken to you.
>
> Remain in me, as I also remain in you. No branch can bear fruit by itself: it must remain in the vine. Neither can you bear fruit unless you remain in me.

In John 15:5–8, Jesus repeats Himself a little but adds a key thought.

> I am the vine; you are the branches. If you remain in me and I in you, you will bear much fruit; apart from me you can do nothing. (Now

for the key thought) If you do not remain in me, you are like a branch that is thrown away and withers; such branches are picked up, thrown into the fire and burned. If you remain in me and my words remain in you, ask whatever you wish and it will be done for you. This is to my Father's glory, that you bear much fruit, showing yourselves to be my disciples.

If you keep my commands, you will remain in my love, just as I have kept my Father's commands and remain in His love. (John 15:10)

Yes, God wanted me to write that song so that I would be able to learn that He did not simply want me to "enlighten others in an entertaining way," but to learn a lesson myself from that song. Looking back, I now know that every song God had me write was not just a song for others but that I too must grow by learning from the lyrics.

When I think back to that hotel room in Kansas City in 1990 when God gave me the answer to my prayer, *You are to enlighten others in an entertaining way*, that answer did not come quickly. I forgot to mention that I had to wait for a while. Now, I realize that God had much in store for my future. The entertaining others about the Bible was only one small part of my work which was to come. He could have answered my prayer like this, for example:

Your first assignment is to enlighten others in an entertaining way. By that I mean I will be giving you songs to write. Yes, I will wake you up in the wee hours of the morning with a new melody that you are to write down so as to not forget it. Then, within a day or two, I will be directing you to the scriptures you are to use as the key to the lyrics.

Now, later, you will be needed to help your son, Mike, pastoring at a nursing home. By the way, that will be the nursing home in which your wife will become a resident. She will eventually pass and join me here in heaven on January 6, 2013.

However, you and Mike will continue to preach at that nursing home way down in southwest Missouri. Yes, I know you now live near St. Louis, but due to the bad economy there, you will be following my direction to move your computer company to southwest Missouri.

There, I will direct you and your wife to attend and sometimes even join various denominations. The reason for this is so you will have a working understanding of the different denominations.

Following your work with your son, you will be preaching at a place to which you will be directed by someone, but not from Me directly.

Finally, I will have you return to writing more songs, but for these new songs, you will use your sermon writing skills to get the lyrics. Jesus and I will hone your sermon writing skills. As you write them, we will be directing you as to which words to use and make it get your lessons across to the congregation better.

Now, I'm not yet done answering your prayer. No, I will also have you write a book about how one goes from a small child and under my guidance and direction to becoming a true disciple of Christ.

Following that, I will have you teach particular individuals whom I will send to you under my direction. You will write letters in some cases. In other cases, the individual will be sent by me to look to you as a disciple and ask you for help in understanding My ways. Now, there is the answer to your prayer about what I want you to do for Me.

You know, I maybe should have just left it off with your first assignment and then add the other assignments as they are needed. Anyway, go to sleep now knowing that I have answered your prayer my child.

Now, my dear readers, you see, I just taught you about God's answers to prayers in an entertaining way. If the potential instructions God could have issued in 1990 were like the one I just gave as an example, that too was an entertaining way of teaching you.

Earlier in this book, I wrote about how we humans say or write something to convey only one thought to the person or persons to whom we are addressing. But God is so much more powerful than that. He uses words that take on multiple meanings. I should have realized long ago that God gave me those early assignments so that

I too would learn from them. They are lessons for my listeners and for me as well.

I now return to the subject of God's rebuke. The song I was instructed to complete was titled "Rebuke: Correction or Condemnation." It comes from various books of the Bible but begins in the book of Proverbs. It continues with the inspired words of the books which were the letters to the early churches.

> Out in the open wisdom calls aloud, she raises her voice in the public square; on top of the wall she cries out, at the city gate she makes her speech: "How long will you who are simple love your simple ways? How long will mockers delight in mockery and fools hate knowledge? Repent at my rebuke! Then I will pour out my thoughts to you, I will make known to you my teachings. But since you refuse to listen when I call and no one pays attention when I stretch out my hand, since you disregard all my advice and do not accept my rebuke, I in tum will laugh when disaster strikes you; I will mock when calamity overtakes you— when calamity overtakes you like a storm, when disaster sweeps over you like a whirlwind, when distress and trouble overwhelm you.

> Then they will call to me but I will not answer; they will look for me but will not find me, since they hated knowledge and did not choose to fear the Lord. Since they would not accept my advice and spurned my rebuke, they will eat the fruit of their ways and be filled with the fruit of their schemes. For the waywardness of the simple will kill them, and the complacency of fools will destroy them; but whoever listens to me will live in safety and be at ease, without fear of harm. (Proverbs 1:20–33)

Now remember, my brothers and sisters, the above quote came from wisdom as the thing God looks for in every human heart. According to the book of Proverbs, those who seek wisdom and keeps it in their hearts so God will see that it is there will benefit greatly as follows:

1. Chapter 1 teaches us the purpose and theme of the entire book. It also gives us a warning against the invitation of sinful men and teaches about wisdom's rebuke which was just stated in the previous quote.

2. Chapter 2 states the many moral benefits of having stored wisdom in our hearts. It states that if you turn your ear to wisdom and apply your heart to understanding and you call out for insight and cry aloud for understanding and look for it and search for it, you will then understand the fear of the *Lord* and find the knowledge of God, for the *Lord* gives wisdom; from His mouth come knowledge and understanding. He also holds success in store for the upright, and He becomes a shield to those whose walk. He is blameless, for He guards the course of the just and protects the way of His faithful ones.

   Those who store wisdom in your hearts, knowledge will be present in your souls. Discretion will also protect you, and understanding will guard you. Wisdom will save you from the ways of the wicked. Wisdom will save you from the adulterous woman by recognizing her seductive words. With wisdom, you will walk in the ways of the good and keep on the paths of the righteous. Unlike the immoral and wicked ones, you will find favor in God.

3. Chapter 3 states that wisdom bestows well-being. With wisdom, your life will be prolonged, and you will win favor and a good name in the sight of both God and man. Do not be wise in your own eyes because the Lord God shuns evil. Honor the Lord with your wealth, with the first fruits. Most of all, do not resent His rebuke because He rebukes

the ones He loves in order to correct them and not condemn them. There are so many benefits you will receive in life because of the favor of the Lord God.

4. Chapter 4 tells us that you must seek and store wisdom in your heart at all cost, for wisdom will teach you how to recognize the evildoers so that you can avoid them because they cannot rest until they do evil. Give careful thought to the paths of righteousness.

5. Chapter 5 once again warns us against adultery. Not only is adultery one of the don'ts in the Ten Commandments but it shows that you did not seek, find, and store wisdom in your heart.

6. According to the dictionary, folly is the lack of sense and shows foolishness. It is the foolish acts and/or beliefs on one's part. It is a foolish and senseless undertaking. In chapter 6, we learn the warnings against folly. Wisdom must be kept and followed in order to keep from straying toward the acts of folly. By shaking hands in pledge with a stranger, you have been trapped by what you said, ensnared by the words of your mouth. Once again, this chapter like those before it warns against the acts of adultery. Remember you must not fall for the trickery of those who practice lustfulness. It goes as far as to say the one who commits adultery has no sense and it will destroy himself and he will stand to lose one's home, and the jealousy of a husband's fury will show no mercy, and there will be revenge. One comment here that I learned many years ago, in the state of Georgia, adultery is against the law and any military service personnel who commits adultery stands to be dishonorably discharged.

7. Chapter 7 continues with the warnings against the adulterous woman. Men should not fall for their wicked ways. They have a sharp tongue that unless you recognize their wickedness, you just might fall for their trickery and commit adultery. It is my understanding therefore that a man

has a difficult time keeping on the right path that wisdom teaches and is prone to stray onto the wrong path simply because of the ways of the wicked women.

8. Chapter 8 talks about wisdom's call. It states that wisdom calls out aloud, and I quote:

> To you, O people, I call out; I raise my voice to all mankind, you who are simple, gain prudence; you who are foolish, set your hearts on it. Listen, for I have trustworthy things to say; I open my lips to speak what is right. My mouth speaks what is true, for my lips detest wickedness.

There is much we can learn but too much to include in this book.

9. Chapter 9 compares the invitations of both wisdom and folly.

The list goes on, and I cannot comment on the importance of all thirty-one chapters of Proverbs. I tried to address those which teach specifically about the importance of having wisdom in your heart.

You may be asking yourself why there is so much attention to the subject of one keeping wisdom in their heart when this section is about God's rebuke. Well, they are related. In the Old Testament, it was wisdom that guided righteous people to stay on the right paths of life. Because of the New Testament, we learn important lessons about what we should do and not do by reading the teachings of Jesus and the letters to the early churches written by those who were the first disciples of Christ Jesus. In the book of Acts, we learn that the Holy Spirit descended on the disciples and gave them the same powers Jesus had while He was on earth. So those who say we do not have to obey the things written by the disciples because they were not the words of Jesus Himself are wrong. Correction! Since the Holy

Spirit gave the disciples the same powers as Jesus, then their words are just as important as those spoken by God's only Son, Jesus!

It was the Gnostics who tried to step into the early Christian churches and teach their wicked beliefs. There were and still will be false prophets. Jesus warned us against their trickery and evilness. The book of Proverbs was written before Jesus came to earth to teach us and to begin to gather people whom God would be proud to call His own. These people are the ones Jesus refers to as the "children of light." He does so because they live in the light and not in the dark.

Yet there will always be those evil ones who stay in the dark world and hate those of us who live in the light. Therefore, we must now listen to the lessons taught by God and His only Son and those of the disciples. We must listen to their lessons even if some lessons involve their rebuke. We must see their rebuke as their direct lessons from which we must learn. Their rebuke is a way of guiding us away from a path that we may have taken which is the same wrong path talked about in the book of Proverbs.

Just because we now have direct guidance from Jesus by reading the New Testament does not mean we should forget the importance of our need to seek wisdom, store it, and keep it in our hearts so that when God looks into the hearts of everyone, righteous and unrighteous, He will find those who have wisdom. When He sees that we are straying away from wisdom's teachings and the teachings of Jesus, we receive either minor guidance or rebuke. Minor guidance is a term I use and is not found in the Bible. I see minor guidance as something we receive when we listen to God and are able to follow His directions. However, when we stray in a more serious manner, then God must rebuke us because He loves us. He does not rebuke us because He hates us and wants to condemn us. *No!* He rebukes us to guide us in a direction or path that He wants us to follow.

We should also be aware that God warns us not to harden our hearts because He rebuked us. He loves His children, and like our earthly fathers, we receive rebuke because He loves us and wants us to not go astray.

I see this as probably the most important lesson we can learn today. Our culture is falling apart because fathers are leaving the family for a younger wife. Fathers are leaving the family because their wife wants a different husband. Remember, my dear friends, my brothers and sisters, divorce is not something that Jesus took lightly. Why? Because the father's primary job in the family is to be the source of spiritual guidance to all family members. He is to lead the family not as a dictator but as a loving leader who wants the same thing for his family as God wants. He speaks for God. The children should especially take heed of their father's teachings when it comes to what is right and what is wrong. This is the spiritual teaching for which every father is responsible.

Why did God direct me to be a disciple? I really don't know why He picked me; but He knew my spirit, my soul, even before He created His wonderful universe. So much for the accidental creation of the universe.

As the result of not listening to God, not having righteous fathers in the family to whom the family should listen, we now have chaos! The chaos starts in the family and then spreads to the community. In our country, it then spreads to the county, followed by the state, and ultimately ends up in our country's culture. Oh, now you see the main topic of this book—the fact that there is a battle going on between the holy scriptures of the Bible and our culture. If we allow our culture to drift into the world of darkness, we are in deep trouble with our Creator. In the early days of the United States of America, a new town would seek a pastor to guide them, and the building of a church was one of the main things that must be done ASAP! We also now look back and see the dark world try to disrupt this by introducing the saloons and the evil bad guys who kill simply for the sake of killing.

It was the wish of those early folks that righteousness would overcome evilness. In addition to the hymn that teaches us the fact that we have a powerful foe in the evil one, Satan, also that hymn talks about the fact that God is a bulwark.

We know the faults of socialism. They viscously put down all religions, burn the churches, and murder Christian pastors. Then the second attack comes from the hate that exists in the dark world. We have people committing mass murder in our schools and places of worship, and the age of the attackers has no limit. Children are not being parented by those who believe in Jesus and have no spiritual guidance at home. Oh, they claim they teach their children right from wrong, but that is not enough. The teaching must come from a spiritual source. Missouri now has a bill to allow using the Holy Bible in the classroom which is a tremendous turnaround from what we have seen in recent years. The socialists want to do away with the mention of God in any government building and on our money. I know I mentioned that earlier, but it deserves a second look. They seem to forget that the separation of church and state in our constitution is because the kingdoms of Europe had strict control over the Christian church. The church was under government rule. It was not placed in our constitution to keep the church from interfering with the government. The Bible tells us that God will continue to bless those nations that worship Him.

The youth today do not know the truth about rebuke. They see it as a personal attack on their rights. The ACLU has that same train of thought. The youth are not ruled, not taught about the importance of the Spirit. They do not believe they have a spirit. They no longer believe in God because they were raised outside the church. They were raised by the culture of the dark world: the dark world of the evil ones—the ones we are taught to stay clear of in the book of Proverbs and all the other books in the Bible. As Jesus warned, *those who live in the dark world will see all good and righteousness as foolishness for they do not know where they are going.* To them the Bible is foolishness. To them, those who preach what the Bible teaches are mere foolish. The belief in God and also in Jesus is foolishness. They don't believe in the statement "For God so loved the world that He gave His only Son so that whosoever believes in Him will not perish but have everlasting life." They don't believe in Jesus's statement in John 14:6–7:

> I am the truth and the life. No one comes to
> the Father except through me. If you really know

me, you will know my Father as well. From now
on, you do know him and have seen him.

They do not believe in Jesus's teaching of Nicodemus in John
3:3–7, when Jesus replied:

> Very truly I tell you, no one can see the
> kingdom of God unless they are born again. Very
> truly I tell you, no one can enter the kingdom of
> God unless they are born of water and the Spirit.
> Flesh gives birth to flesh, but the Spirit gives
> birth to spirit. You should not be surprised at my
> saying, 'you must be born again.

Our modern culture sees these truths as foolishness yet believes
in murdering babies even after the time of their birth. How much
more evil can a society get? That is the culture that will take over
our country and the entire world unless we have disciples to teach all
people the truth. God's disciples need to preach outside the church as
well as inside. Now I see why God wanted this book to be published.

Today God sent the message to me that I am a disciple and
not simply an ordained independent minister or nondenominational
pastor. I am no longer needed in the assisted living place. I am needed
to preach to anyone who is having spiritual problems. They want
guidance and do not know where to go. Due to the constant arguing
about minor details concerning the writings in the Bible, many who
want to find out the truth do not trust the official church. Now I am
in no way teaching that people no longer attend or become a member of the structured church. No, I simply want to tell those churches
who are governed by a superior organizational head to stop the arguing. Concentrate your preaching on Jesus. Remember what Jesus said
in Revelations, *I hold this against you. You have forgotten your first love.*

As an independent minister and official disciple, I say we
Christian clergy should concentrate on teaching directly from the
Bible *only!* We should not let the differences between the organized

churches enter into our teaching. I pray that the organized churches also quit the arguing and stick to the true teaching of the inspired words in the Bible.

Even when individuals read a scripture for a second or third time and come away with a slightly different meaning, they should realize that God has the ability to word things with multiple meanings. Who is so superior to God that they think they should argue about what the inspired words of our Creator mean and that all people should understand the meaning the same way they do?

As a nondenominational preacher and also a disciple, I believe in simply stating what the Bible says and allowing each person to come away with their interpretation. I'm not perfect, but I do believe that God wants me to preach outside the formal church in order to try to put a stop to the evil dark world from capturing the souls of those who just might listen to someone they can trust. God wants me to forget about preaching to a formal church congregation. I am to preach to the individuals who want to know the truth and want to be saved if what they heard Jesus say is the truth.

God and His glorious Son, Jesus, are perfect and cannot lie. Therefore, we must trust the words God inspired in the Bible. We clergy must use great caution in our additional comments. Both Proverbs and Revelations have the warning about adding to or subtracting from the words of the scroll. Whoever does so must answer to God for their wrongdoing. They will receive the reward which their actions deserve.

In one of the churches God directed my wife and me to join, we heard the pastor announce repeatedly about the addition of new members. However, he somehow did not notice the greater number of people leaving the church. Had he realized the truth, he would have taken appropriate action to find out what he or others in the church were doing wrong. People leave for only two main reasons: 1) They do not like the teachings of the pastor. 2) They do not like how others in the church, either laypersons, teachers, or the general members of the congregation, treat them.

A different church my wife and I were directed by God to attend had the pastor's son who came home for a visit preach about how when you attend church services you must wear your best clothes. Jesus said, *Do not worry about the clothes you put on your body.* There are people in this part of the state who cannot afford real nice clothes. They wear what they have. When a preacher rebukes them about their clothes, he is driving people away. Are only those who make a lot of money and can afford expensive clothing should attend? Is this because they would be able to put more money in the collection plate? That may very well be the feeling visitors come away with. My wife and I never returned to that church.

Not all churches God sent us to attend or join had wrong teachings. God wanted us to experience both good and bad preaching. That was just one part of my training in order to become the disciple God has desired me to be from the time even before I was born. God selects the soul or spirit He wants for each embryo. Who then has the right to terminate something God has put into place so that His will shall prevail?

In my ending, I would like to thank God for His guidance and training. I feel I was too slow to catch on to His divine intent. But, like I said, I am not perfect. None of us are. We are all sinners and have no business looking down on those who want to know the truth but don't know where to go to find out what the truth is. I would love to help anyone who lives in the dark world now to turn away from the dark and find out what pleases the Lord God and decide to be born again so their sins can be forgiven. Additionally, I would like to continue to teach them that being born again is not the end. They are expected to bear much fruit and grow as a Christian and become a disciple themselves. I ask these things in Jesus's name. Amen.

There Is More to Be Learned from the Whole Bible

A Summary of Scripture vs. Culture

What I want to do in this chapter is to repeat some things already stated. I do this because it is a way of summarizing what this book is about: scripture vs. culture.

Before I begin this most severely outspoken chapter, I wish to inform you that one morning, when I thought I was done with writing this book at the end of chapter 8, God gave me an order. I was to tune into CBN, the Christian Broadcasting Network, and listen to the conversation already in progress. It was through listening to the broadcast and listening to God at the same time that I came up with the primary topic of chapter 9.

I do not wish to offend anyone; but due to my lifelong relationship with the Holy Trinity and having been guided and directed all through my life by our wonderful, loving, and kind God, I cannot help but pass on the main thing I learned. I almost forgot to mention it in the first eight chapters, but God made sure the book He ordered me to write ended with one final but most important topic. I'm sorry if I offend you, but here it is.

It used to be that it was the other countries in the "world" which the Bible refers to as the "dark world" that had the cultural problems. The Bible teaches us to not love the "world." This statement in the Bible was mentioned in earlier chapters if you recall. The introduction of those from the dark world caused our own country to become more like them than the great United States of America. If we kept it up in trying to be fair and equitable to all from every corner of the "world," we risked infecting our country with nonbelievers, with those who hate anything to do with our religious values. Jesus taught us in His own words written in John 15:18–25, and I quote:

> If the world hates you, keep in mind that it hates me first. If you belonged to the world, it would love you as its own. As it is, you do not belong to the world, but I have chosen you out of the world. That is why the world hates you. Remember what I told you. A servant is not greater than his master. If they persecuted me they will persecute you also. If they will treat you this way because of my name, for they do not know the one who sent me. If I had not come and spoken to them, they would not be guilty of sin; but now they have no excuse for their sin. Whoever hates me hates my Father as well. If I had not done among them the works, no one else did, they would not be guilty of sin. As it is, they have seen and yet they have hated both me and my Father. But this is to fulfill what is written in their Law. They hated me without reason.

I would like to continue giving additional lessons from Jesus with the words written in John 12:35–36:

> You are going to have the light just a little while longer. Walk while you have the light, before darkness overtakes you. Whoever walks in the dark does not know where they are going. Believe in the light while you have the light, so that you may become children of light.

Then I would like to add more of the lessons from Jesus, in Ephesians 5:8–11:

> For you were once darkness, but now you are light in the Lord. Live as children of light (for the fruit of the light consists in all goodness, righteousness and truth) and find out what pleases the Lord. Have nothing to do with the fruitless deeds of darkness, but rather expose them.

If we had stuck with the countries from which our ancestors originally came, we could have remained a people with those values.

President Trump is doing his best to make our country great again as he promised. He has made many great strides, but the other party has put up a series of blockades. I personally believe the other political party has switched from the party of John Fitzgerald Kennedy and others to a party that wants socialism which actually is a euphemism for communism. They have even chosen to call themselves by a different name. They now say they are the "Progressive Democrats." They do not say to where they are progressing. The term "progressing" means they are moving in a different direction. Why don't they tell everyone what that direction is?

Remember what the USSR, one of the world's worse evil empires, actually was. It was the United Soviet Socialist Republic. If we become socialists, we will also be the new USSR, United States Socialist Republic.

However, socialism is not our only problem. The problem with the unkind and unwanted change in our country's society actually began when we well intended to help those who came from countries where you could not work hard and keep your nose clean and then easily prosper. Oh! Wait one minute! Is not the Democratic Party fighting tooth and nail to let those who storm our southern border enter our country?

Remember the terrorists who kill our people, including Christians and Muslims who do not become radicalized, were responsible for the destruction of the World Trade Center in New York City on September 11, 2001. They also brag about other events they have caused.

They now say they are joining in with those from the countries south of the United States. They admit that they are pretending to be from those countries south of us with the intention to do great harm within our borders. They can and do cause the storm of people at our southern border by the hundreds of thousands each month so it makes it almost impossible to detect who is a radicalized terrorist and who is an honest Mexican or other southern person with our same values but lives in a country where those values get them nowhere.

Our country was founded on the Christian-Judeo principles. That means the values from the Holy Bible. Not to change the subject, but we must remember that there are Jews who have converted directly to Christianity and Jews who saw that the genealogy from David down to Jesus was accurate and that Jesus is the Messiah. They call themselves the Messianic Jews.

However, we then invited everyone from all over the world, or the "dark world" as the Bible puts it, to come into our country and join us in becoming prosperous. We forgot to check and see what their country's methods were to become prosperous. We introduced those who did not believe in God, let alone Jesus or even the loving and kind values we learned from our ancestors. Yes, we caused much of our culture's damage ourselves. We were well intended but ended up hurting ourselves. When you create a wonderful loving, caring society, it is probably best not to invite those who hate such values to come and join us in our wonderland of peace and prosperity. When Jesus ordered His disciples to go out into the world and preach, He told them that if they did not want to listen, they should simply wipe the dust off their sandals and move on. You cannot be a disciple to a full nation or even a large group of people from such nations. It is best to tackle Jesus's orders to His disciples a few people at a time.

There are exceptions to that suggestion, though. When some of our world's best evangelists like Billy Graham went among the third world countries and preached, they were successful in converting thousands to Christianity in one night, in one meeting, in one event of evangelistic preaching. Our government was not intended nor even good at trying to be evangelists. The United States government was not created to do that. Like many say, "That's not my job."

Maybe it would be nice if the heads of our government had the type of values our forefathers had when we became a nation; it would be much better off. A president that was not from within the existing government might help. A billionaire who listened closely to preachers of various denominations would be great. Why, he could possibly turn this country back into the kind of country our forefathers intended to create. Yes, I'm talking about President Trump. I believe God saw to it that he was put in the oval office. You may not be aware of it, but every morning President Trump holds a prayer meeting with members of various denominations. I was invited to join from a distance. That is, from my home, I could offer input for the president to consider and even offer a prayer for the whole meeting to read aloud. *Wow*! I not only saw that invitation as a privilege but an honor.

It is written in Genesis 12:1–3 what God told Abram (before God renamed him Abraham):

> Now the Lord had said to Abram: Get out of your country, from your family and from your father's house. To a land that I will show you. I will make you a great nation (we know as Israel); I will bless you and make your name great: and you shall be a blessing. I will bless those who bless you and I will curse him who curses you. And in you all the families of the earth shall be blessed.

With those words directly from God, it is no wonder President Trump moved the United States Embassy from Tel Aviv to Jerusalem which is the biblical capital of the Israelites.

You may not have heard via the fake news networks that the small United States Embassy that was already in Jerusalem did not report to the United States government. No, it reported directly to the enemies of Israel. By taking the embassy away from the enemies and having this embassy become the main embassy in Israel, President Trump did both the United States and Israel a great favor. It was the right move by a righteous person. Those in the Democratic Party who opposed this move show where their beliefs are centered. I am now writing these words under the direction and guidance of both God and Jesus to whom God gave all power and control over all of His creation, for Jesus even said that He was with God even before the creation.

You see, God created the state of Israel and intended for it to be great. If you don't believe me, please consider believing God Who wrote those words in Genesis 12:1–3. God cannot lie. Jesus cannot lie. Therefore, all that they state is the absolute truth, the whole truth, and nothing but the truth.

It is refreshing to see the small towns still going to church and doing their best to try to be more like Jesus. Jesus said that nobody will see the kingdom of God except through Him. He is the light of the world, and people prefer to stay in the dark world and hate all that has to do with the light. They even hate the people who live in the light. They simply do not know where they are going. If you do not believe me, please read the teachings of Jesus. He cannot lie.

Until we can get the majority of the population to live in the light, we will see our country and our culture go quite possibly and quite literally to hell. We can't say who goes to hell. That would be judging. But the Bible tells us that outside the vine, outside the light, you may not be allowed to enter heaven.

Our country needs more disciples. Our preachers should be more concerned with preaching directly from the Bible rather than the petty arguments brought up at the denominations' headquarters. The protestant denominations are following the footsteps of the Vatican. I don't want to sound like I am criticizing the Catholic Church, but they are doing the same things as the protestant denominations' headquarters. The preachers should be running things. When a preacher begins to turn to the dark world and lust takes over, there should be a sudden firing of the preacher, and one who is righteous replaces that preacher.

Is any of this possible, or are we too far down the track to be able to reverse things in the churches? We are too far down the track when it comes to the people who guide the culture.

Please use your power and freedom to vote; before, all the freedoms and things that made this country great once came from the original constitution and all the amendments that followed. If we listen to those who want to do away with our current constitution, then all our freedoms are gone, gone forever possibly. That means all of the amendments from the time George Washington was president until today are thrown out. We no longer have the freedom of speech, the freedom of religion, the freedom to bear arms, and the freedom to do all the things the constitution and the amendments bestowed upon us.

Seriously, please use your power to vote. Please vote to keep our country great. Please vote to keep us blessed by God. Every president says at the end of their State of the Union Address, "God bless you and God bless America." If we go down the path a certain political party wants, I believe we will no longer be blessed by God. If you are a believer, please pray for our government and those whom we have appointed to lead us. May God bless America.

CHAPTER 10

How Can We Correct
What Is Happening

I would like to explain what we must know and then what we must do to spot our country from going deeper into a pit of evil. As a business major in college, I learned that to solve any problem, it is best to first address all the details. Without examining all the details, one cannot solve the problem. Therefore, it is best that I now present all the problems with our society and the cause of each problem in detail. It is a little like spreading evidence on a tabletop so that all the facts are right in front of you in one place so you can study them, examine them, and put them into order of importance. We must first know that what we are trying to fight is the sources that try to change our culture to one that is completely opposite of what is taught by God's inspired words found in the Bible. I call it "scripture vs. culture." Before I spread the facts out onto the tabletop, I would like to point out that anything that is said herein is backed up by God's holy words. I did not make up these things. There are no grounds for anyone to try to take my written evidence to court, unless of course the court is a packed court, if you get what I mean. Here are the facts:

1. For those who may not know it, long before God created the earth and life on the earth, He created the heavens. Genesis said that first God created the heavens. How did that begin? I started to write I was not knowledgeable enough when God corrected me with one scripture. Jesus

said that He was with God even before creation. Therefore, even before God created anything, there was the Holy Trinity: God the Father, God the Son, and God the Holy Spirit. Then he created three archangels. Gabriel was the announcer of important events. He told Abraham that he and his wife would have a child even though they were both very old. Gabriel told Mary that she would give birth to Jesus. He also told Joseph what was about to happen and that he should marry the Virgin Mary. He announced the birth of Jesus to the shepherds in the fields. There are too many Gabriel announcements to list. Next, there was Michael whom I named my son after. Michael was the fighter of all that was evil. He conducted the battles for God. Finally, there was the problem child, Lucifer, a.k.a. Satan, a.k.a. Diablo, a.k.a. the devil, a.k.a. the evil one.

2. Satan wants to be worshipped by the humans God created but does not have even one ounce of love for anything God created except himself. He hates even those whom he wishes to have worship him.

3. Satan knows he cannot win the battle against God, but he enjoys trying to destroy anything related to God's work. He especially takes great pleasure in destroying people's lives and people's culture. For our purpose of battling Satan, we must now concentrate on his destruction of our culture.

4. There are three very prominent places where Satan has made progress in his attempt to destroy our culture:

   a. Firstly, there is the movie industry. As time passes, we see movies introducing more cultural problems but presenting them as being normal. For example, the language in movies has gotten to a point where every other word is foul language. The movie producers have been convinced by Satan that they must present the true current culture in their movies. If that is true, then how come those movies produced by Christian filmmakers are so popular without even one foul word? Why is it that they can produce a movie showing a normal family environment as normal and not a dysfunctional family as being normal? Hollywood now tries to tell us that two mothers or two fathers are normal. This has spread to our family time shows on television. These shows now introduce dysfunctional families as being normal. Even children's cartoons now have dysfunctional families portrayed as being normal.

b. Our own government is the second source of falsehood. They pass laws that we cannot show sexual immorality as evil. We cannot discriminate against the LGBTQ society. We must allow babies to be killed at the time of birth or shortly after. Judges block those laws from states that say abortions must not be performed once a heartbeat is detected or that life begins at the time of conception as the words of God say. Those in government offices who fight for righteousness are fought without mercy by those who call themselves "Progressive Democrats." They are also fought without mercy by judges who were appointed by "Progressive Democrats."

c. There is the "fake news media." Like the Progressive Democrats, they report only those things that the Progressive Democrats want to have reported—all the bad things but none of the good things the righteousness lawmakers and heads of government have accomplished. Many of you may remember the independent study commonly called the 88/12 study. In that study, a nonbiased group found that mainstream media and their cable news affiliates all reported the same exact percentages for and against our political parties. That is, 88 percent of the time, these fake news media reported either against the Republican Party or for the Democratic Party. They also reported 12 percent of the time for the Republican Party or against the Democratic Party. How can these supposedly independent television networks report exactly the same percentage for and against the political parties? If this happened in a classroom in any school or college, there would be a rise in suspicion beyond belief.

There are the facts, my friends. Now that we know the three main sources of the proliferation of evil in our society, we can now address how to fight them.

1. The movie and evening television industries. We can refuse to buy those evil and anti-good culture movies. We can boycott those theaters that show those movies. If only those who live in the dark world headed by Satan attend, the popularity will diminish. When it comes to the evening television shows, we can refuse to watch them. We can show good sound enjoyable movies via DVDs we purchase. When good movies on DVDs are purchased and not the evil DVD movies, the law of supply and demand will help correct this problem. If we refuse to watch the shows that advocate evil, the ratings for those shows will diminish.

2. When it comes to our government, we can vote in great numbers against the ones who proliferate evil in our culture. We can vote in those who are righteous. When the righteous officials are in power, they will appoint righteous judges and not those who advocate an evil culture. Please vote for those who are righteous! That is our right and obligation. The term obligation is of the greatest importance here.

3. When it comes to the fake news media, we need to tune into those who tell the truth and not lies. We can get our news from the Christian Broadcasting Network, CBN, or from the Daystar television network or from Fox News. In any of these three, you will hear both sides to every story, but you will hear only the truth and not fake news.

I am not perfect. You are not perfect. Only Jesus is perfect. Therefore, do not put too much stock in any reporting of something a righteous person may do or say that he or she wishes they had not done or said. Yes, President Trump, like each of us—no, all of us—is not perfect; but he is doing his best by holding a prayer meeting each morning before any other business is conducted in the oval office. The Progressive Democrats say that he is a racist. If you had listened to CBN News, you would have heard the niece of Dr. Martin Luther King Jr. say that she knows the president and "he is not a racist." If there is one person of color whom you can believe, it is the niece of Dr. Martin Luther King Jr. She would not lie about something as important as that.

Now, for one final word concerning a fourth source of evil in our society, as part of my official ordination process, I took a vow that I would allow same-sex couples to attend any services I conducted. I also took a vow that I would not marry same-sex couples. Now, I would like to present evidence in the form of biblical scripture to address this touchy subject. You will hear some say that the books written in the form of letters to churches and other audiences are not the words of God or Jesus so they are not bound to obey such writings. This is a false belief. Firstly, in the book of Acts, we find that the Holy Spirit came down upon the disciples and gave them the same powers that Jesus had while He was Emanuel, God among us. Additionally, every word in the Holy Bible and even the words I write here are God inspired. I know this because I was about to send my edited copy of chapter 10 to my publisher when God told me to completely replace it with the one you are now reading. Even as I write, I am guided by our heavenly Father about each thought, each sentence, and even each word. God has special words that only He knows their power over other words that seem to say the same thing. *Romans 1:18–32 deals with God's wrath against sinful humanity:*

> The wrath of God is being revealed from
> heaven against all the godlessness and wickedness
> of people, *who suppress the truth by their wick-*

edness, since what may be known about God is plain to them, because God has made it plain to them. For since the creation of the world God's invisible qualities—his eternal power and divine nature—have been clearly seen being understood from what has been made, *so that people are without excuse.*

For although they knew God, they neither glorified him as God nor gave thanks to him, but *their thinking became futile and their foolish hearts were darkened. Although they claimed to be wise, they became fools and exchanged the glory of the immortal God* for images made to look like a mortal human being and birds and animals and reptiles.

Therefore *God gave them over in the sinful desires of their hearts to sexual impurity for the degrading of their bodies with one another. They exchanged the truth about God for a lie,* and worshiped and served created things rather than the Creator—who is forever praised. Amen.

Because of this, *God gave them over to shameful lusts. Even their women exchanged natural sexual relations for unnatural ones. In the same way the men also abandoned natural relations with women and were inflamed with lust for one another. Men committed shameful acts with other men, and received in themselves the due penalty for their error.*

Furthermore, just as they did not think it worthwhile to retain the knowledge of God, so *God gave then over to the depraved mind, so that they do what ought not to be done.* They have become filled with every kind of wickedness, evil, greed and depravity. They are full of envy,

murder, strife, deceit and malice. They are gos-
sips, slanderers, God-haters, insolent arrogant
and boastful; they invent ways of doing evil; *they
disobey their parents; they have no understanding,
no fidelity, no love, no mercy. Although they know
God's righteous decree that those who do such things
deserve death, they not only continue to do these very
things but also approve of those who practice them.*

God could not inspire words any more accurate than this. Well,
since He is God, He may be able to do that; but I believe that He
wanted us all to know the truth. God cannot lie. He can only speak
the truth. Likewise, God can only inspire words that are truthful. If
you think differently, that is your right. However, please be aware
that we are on this earth for a very short period of time compared to
eternity. Please, everyone, ask yourself this question, "Do I pick and
choose what words in the Bible I will adhere to and those I wish to
ignore?" Also, "Do I do as God wants or what my evil-guided mind
wants?" One final question to ask yourself is: "Do I wish to spend
eternity when I leave this earthly life with God or with the evil one
who has absolutely no love for me?"

I pray now that I have at least helped at least one person to wake
up and see the truth. God is the truth. Anything besides God may
be persuaded by the evil one, Satan. Satan does not love you. God
loves you. I love you. I write what God wants me to write. I also write
hoping that because of God's guidance, direction, and training all
through my life, I am doing God's work in the exact way He wants
me to. I am only God's tool, His humble servant. I am not a great
person. I am nothing without God's help. Like everyone else, I am a
sinner. The only difference between me and others like me who live
in the light and those who live in the dark world who want to change
our culture to one completely opposed to God's will is that we believe
in God and that every word in the Bible was inspired by God; we
believe in Jesus as God's only Son, and therefore, we are forgiven. We
are pardoned. We are redeemed.

For you Christians who tend to side with the Progressive Democrats, you need to realize that, like them, you will have to answer to God come your judgment day. Do you feel comfortable with your acts, or do you wish to change your ways to be more in compliance with the wishes of God Almighty, Creator of heaven and earth, and His only begotten Son, Jesus, our Lord? It is He who was conceived by the Holy Spirit, was born of the Virgin Mary, suffered under Pontius Pilate, and was crucified dead and buried. He descended into hell. On the third day, He arose from the dead and ascended into heaven where He sits at the right hand of God Almighty, and He shall come to judge the quick and the dead. Do you believe in the one holy universal Christian church, the forgiveness of sin, and life everlasting? If so, then please reconsider what you are doing. Reconsider what you vote for in Congress. Reconsider the comments you make against the righteous leaders of our government. Our government was founded under God, indivisible, with liberty and justice for all. I ask these things in Jesus's name. Amen.

Here is my final words on the subject of sexual immorality. The two words "sexual immorality" or "sexually immoral" or any other form are listed in the Holy Bible forty-three times. It is often mentioned in the same verse as adulterers, murders, the practice of evil arts, and many more unclean acts that will cause the guilty party to either not be allowed in heaven or have turned away from God. God is in charge. God is the head of His kingdom. He has a perfect right to say whom He will allow in his kingdom and who will not be allowed.

Those preachers, pastors, ministers, reverends, or by any other name who are often referred to as men of God cannot, in my understanding of the Bible, be a member of God's teachers. If they have committed such a great sin as to no longer be in God and God be in them, then how can they be among those who are permitted to enter the kingdom of God when they leave this earth? Remember God never turns away from those who are his children, the children of light because they live in the light. If a child of God chooses, by their own free will to turn away from God and prefer to live in the dark world which is headed by Satan and his demonic beings, then they, the children who lived in the light, are now part of and live in the dark world with the evildoers.

Yet, they are not lost completely; if they take it upon themselves to be back in God's good graces, they can be with God once more. They can confess their sins of the dark world and ask for God's forgiveness one more time. God loves them, but they have shown that they no longer love God. God will accept them back if they truly want to come back to God with all their hearts, all their souls, and all their minds. That means, though, that they must give up their evil life and go back to acting like children of light once more.

So that you don't think I am making all this up, I now list the most important entries which put sexual immorality in with the other major sins and what God has to say about them.

First Corinthians 5:9–13 contains such entries:

> I wrote to you in my letter not to associate with sexually immoral people—not at all meaning the people of this world who are immoral, or the greedy and swindlers, or idolaters. In that case you would have to leave this world. But now I am writing to you that you must not associate with anyone who claims to be a brother or sister but is sexually immoral or greedy, and idolater or slanderer, a drunkard or swindler. Do not even eat with such people.

> What business is it of mine to judge those outside the church? Are you not to judge those inside? God will judge those outside. "Expel the wicked person from among you."

Then in 1 Corinthians 6:9, Paul wrote:

> Or do you not know that wrongdoers will not inherit the kingdom of God? Do not be

deceived: Neither the sexually immoral nor idolaters nor adulterers nor men who have sex with men nor thieves nor the greedy nor drunkards nor slanderers nor swindlers will inherit the kingdom of God.

I would like to mention now that Paul continued with a complete lesson on sexual immorality beginning with verses 12 through 20, which concludes his entire chapter 6.

Ephesians 5:3 states:

But among you there must not be even a hint of sexual immorality, or of any kind of impurity, or of greed because these are improper for God's holy people.

In Ephesians 5:5, it is written:

For of this you can be sure; No immoral, impure or greedy person—such a person is an idolater—has any inheritance in the kingdom of Christ and of God.

In 1 Timothy 1:9, it is written:

We also know that the law is made not for the righteous but the for the lawbreakers and rebels, the ungodly and sinful, the unholy and irreligious, for those who kill their fathers or mothers, for murderers, for the sexually immoral, for those practicing homosexuality, for slave traders and liars and perjurers—and for whatever else is contrary to the sound doctrine that conforms to the gospel concerning the glory of the blessed God, which he entrusted to me.

See that no one is sexually immoral, or is godless like Esau, who from a single meal sold his inheritance rights as the oldest son. (Hebrews 12:16)

Marriage should be honored by all, and the marriage bed kept pure, for God will judge the adulterer and all the sexually immoral. (Hebrews 13:4)

Those who are victorious will inherit all this, and I will be their God and they will be my children. But the cowardly, the unbelieving, the vile, the murderers the sexually immoral, those who practice magic arts, the idolaters and all liars— they will be consigned to the fiery lake of burning sulfur. This is the second death. (Revelation 21:7–8)

In Revelation 22:14–15, also Jesus Himself states:

Blessed are those who wash their robes, that they may have the right to the tree of life and may go through the gates into the city. Outside are the dogs, those who practice magic arts, the sexually immoral, the murderers, the idolaters and everyone who loves and practices falsehood.

Even in the Old Testament, we find in Numbers 25:1 this statement:

While Israel was staying in Shittim, the men began to indulge in sexual immorality with Moabite women who invited them to the sacrifices to their gods. The people ate the sacrificial meal and bowed down before these gods. So,

Israel yoked themselves to the Baal of Peor. And the Lord's anger burned against them.

In Matthew 5:32, Jesus says this:

> But I tell you that anyone who divorces his wife except for sexual immorality, makes her the victim of adultery, and anyone who marries a divorced woman commits adultery.

In Matthew 15:19, Jesus also says:

> For one of the heart come evil thoughts—murder, adultery, sexual immorality, theft, false testimony, slander. These are what defile a person; but eating with unwashed hands does not defile them.

In Matthew 19:9, Jesus says:

> I tell you that anyone who divorces his wife except for sexual immorality, and marries another woman commits adultery.

In Mark 7:21–23, Jesus is once more speaking:

> For it is from within, out of a person's heart, that evil thoughts come—sexual immorality, theft, murder, adultery, greed, malice, deceit, lewdness, envy, slander, arrogance and folly. All these evils come from inside and defile a person.

I would like to remind you that in the book of Acts, the Holy Spirit, one-third of the Holy Trinity, came down upon the apostles and gave them the same powers that Jesus had while He was among us on earth.

Therefore, in Acts 15:19–21, we read:

> It is my judgment, therefore, that we should not make it difficult for the Gentiles who are turning to God. Instead we should write to them, telling them to abstain from food polluted by idols, from sexual immorality, from the eating of strangled animals and from blood. For the law of Moses has been preached in every city from the earliest times and is read in the synagogues on every Sabbath.

In Acts 15:29, we read:

> You are to abstain from food sacrificed to idols, from blood, from the meat of strangled animals and from sexual immorality. You will do well to avoid these things.

Finally, in Acts 21:25, we read:

> As for the Gentile believers, we have written to them our decision that they should abstain from food sacrificed to idols, from blood, from the meat of strangled animals and from sexual immorality.

I do realize that in the book of Acts, there are things that are repetitious; but if that be the case, then it must be because it is of the utmost importance, and we should be aware that it is of utmost importance.

In Romans, there is only one mention of sexual immorality:

> Let us behave decently, as in the daytime, not in carousing and drunkenness, not in sexual immorality and debauchery, not in dissension and jealousy. Rather clothe yourselves with the Lord Jesus Christ, and do not think about how to gratify the desires of the flesh. (Romans 13:13–14)

That is an extremely powerful one!

In 1 Corinthians 5:1, Paul wrote:

> It is actually reported that there is sexual immorality among you, and of a kind that even pagans do not tolerate: A man is sleeping with his father's wife.
>
> You say, "Food for the stomach and the stomach for food, and God will destroy them both." The body, however, is not meant for sexual immorality but for the Lord, and the Lord for the body. (1 Corinthians 6:13)
>
> Flee from sexual immorality. All other sins a person commits are outside the body, but whoever sins sexually, sins against their own body. Do you not know that your bodies are temples of the Holy Spirit, who is in you, whom you have received from God? You are not your own; you were bought at a price. Therefore, honor God with your bodies. (1 Corinthians 6:18–19)
>
> But since sexual immorality is occurring, each man should have sexual relations with his own wife, and each woman with her own husband. (1 Corinthians 7:2)

We should not commit sexual immorality, as some of them did—and in one day twenty-three thousand of them died. We should not test Christ, as some of them did—and were killed by snakes. (1 Corinthians 10:8–9)

The acts of the flesh are obvious; sexual immorality, impurity and debauchery; idolatry and witchcraft; hatred discord, jealousy, fits of rage, selfish ambition, dissensions, factions and envy; drunkenness, orgies, and the like. I warn you, as I did before, that those who live like this will not inherit the kingdom of God. (Galatians 5:19)

Put to death, therefore whatever belongs to your earthly nature; sexual immorality, impurity, lust, evil desires and greed, which is idolatry. Because of these, the wrath of God is coming. You used to walk in these ways, in the life you once lived. But now you must also rid yourselves of all such things as filthy language from your lips. Do not lie to each other, since you have taken off your old self with its practices and have put on the new self, which is being renewed in knowledge in the image of its Creator. (Colossians 3:5–10)

It is God's will that you should be sanctified; that you should avoid sexual immorality; that each of you should learn to control your own body in a way that is holy and honorable, not in passionate lust like the pagans, who do not know God; and that in this matter no one should wrong or take advantage of a brother or sister... (1 Thessalonians 4:3–6)

For certain individuals whose condemnation was written about long ago have secretly slipped in among you. They are ungodly people,

who pervert the grace of our God into a license
for immorality and deny Jesus Christ our only
Sovereign and Lord. (Jude 4)

In a similar way, Sodom and Gomorrah and
the surrounding towns gave themselves up to sexual immorality and perversion. They serve as an
example of those who suffer the punishment of
eternal fire. (Jude 7)

You cannot get any plainer that that! It states in simple-to-un-
derstand language that those who insist on continuing their ways
of sexual immorality risk suffering the same ending as those who
committed sexual immorality in Sodom and Gomorrah and their
surrounding towns. God destroyed them.

In Revelations, there are four different references to sexual
immorality. Three of them are in chapter 2 and one in chapter 9. In
Revelation 2:14-21, Jesus was speaking to John whom he brought up
into heaven via spirit:

Nevertheless, I have a few things against
you: There are some among you who hold to the
teaching of Balaam, who taught Balak to entice
the Israelites to sin so that they ate food sacrificed to idols and committed sexual immorality.
Likewise, you also have those who hold to the
teaching of the Nicolaitans. Repent therefore!
Otherwise, I will soon come to you and will
fight against them with the sword of my mouth.
Whoever has ears, let them hear what the Spirit
says to the churches. To the one who is victorious, I will give some of the hidden manna. I will
also give that person a white stone with a new
name written on it, known only to the one who
receives it.

To the angel of the church of Thyatira write:

These are the words of the Son of God, whose eyes are like blazing fire and whose feet are like burnished bronze. I know your deeds, your love and faith, your service and perseverance, and that you are now doing more than you did at first.

Nevertheless, I have this against you: You tolerate that woman Jezebel, who calls herself a prophet. By her teaching she misleads my servants into sexual immorality and the eating of food sacrificed to idols. I have given her time to repent of her immorality, but she is unwilling.

Nor did they repent of their murders, their magic arts, their sexual immorality or their thefts. (Revelation 9:21)

I think I have pointed out what the scriptures have to say about sexual immorality. Now you can compare what is quoted above with what is happening in our culture. Movies, television shows, product commercials, and even cartoons are openly displaying sexual immorality almost constantly. It is hard to find even one show or movie or commercial that does not join in with the evil culture into which we are beginning to evolve. That is a shame. How can we also pass laws that state we are not to discriminate against such evilness? It was quoted from the scriptures above that we are to have nothing to do with such people, yet our culture and laws are demanding we not only accept them but accept the evil acts they commit.

This, my dear friends, is my final word on the subject. May God bless you, and may His inspired words in this book help to fight against the evil culture we are now becoming. Do not be fooled into thinking that this new way of thinking is the right way or is completely acceptable. As a nondenominational preacher, I do not believe in gay or lesbian pastors in our churches. I preach strictly from the Bible, and if you do not like my preaching, then you also do not like the teachings of the Bible. There is no question about it; you must obey God and His only Son Christ Jesus. For your own sake, please do so. If you have strayed away, the biblical quotations above mentioned that you do have one last chance. *You must repent.* God loves you, and so do I. I pray for those who have not yet seen the light and have been fooled into thinking by false teachers that what they are doing is against God. Because God loves you, He wants you to come back and welcome Him once more into your body, his temple. He, Jesus, and the Holy Spirit will readily return if you repent and turn away from the dark world which is headed by Satan and his demonic beings, the fallen angles who left heaven with him.

I was born on September 19, 1943, in St. Louis, Missouri. Born into a dysfunctional family, God saw to it that I would be adopted by a good Christian family. I was raised as a true Christian in this family. At the age of accountability, I attended two years of confirmation classes and confirmed by vowing that I believe in God the Father and confess that I am a sinner and ask for His forgiveness. I acknowledge that Jesus is the one and only Son of God the Father and that I want to follow Him, making Him my personal Lord and Savior. I attended Sunday school every Sunday as a child and then church services as an adult.

As a young man in my teens, I became an accomplished musician. I also founded the Ray Scott Trio and performed professionally.

At the same time, I performed in competitions before large audiences. I began writing songs at age fourteen and still continue even today at age seventy-five. I began teaching music at Ludwig Aeolian Studios in St. Louis at age seventeen. I primarily taught accordion but also substituted for other teachers on piano, organ, guitar, and drums. This would become an important factor upon taking on assignments for our Father in heaven.

I served in the United States Navy during the Vietnam War and as a result would later become disabled.

My working career was in computer software design, development, and support. Upon becoming totally disabled, I began my work assignments for our heavenly Father.

During a period of deep depression because my world was falling down around me, I prayed for God to let me know what His plan was for me. His answer was, *You are to enlighten others in an entertaining way.* I took that to mean that I was to do something with my gift of musical talent to enlighten others about the gospel.

Then He had me write songs of which He gave me the melodies upon waking me in the middle of the night. Then I followed His instructions to write music notation so as to not forget the melody. Within a day or two of receiving these new melodies from God, I was directed to the scriptures which were to be used as the lyrics. I then followed his instructions to record and self-produce a CD of songs from God.

My next assignment from our Father was to act as an associate pastor with my already ordained son. We preached at a nursing home where my mother was to spend the rest of her life. God wanted to let those who were residents and were not born again to hear the truth in the gospels. That way they would have a last chance before passing to join God's army and to have nothing to do with the dark world of the evil one.

I believe that God allowed Satan to convince the activities director at the nursing home to fire my son and me and replace our church service with a secular musical talent program. My son and I both wondered what God had in store for us. We knew by then that we're called to do God's work.

My son was given the assignment of going to different nursing homes in more of a chaplain's capacity. He could preach to individuals rather than a congregation. I was directed to preach at an assisted living establishment. I held the Sunday evening service for the residents. As a resident myself, I was concerned that I would be disobeying God if I left assisted living. I was having troubles with the way my medications were issued; and also, I realized I could not afford, financially, to continue living there. However, the management wanted me to continue preaching.

None of the preaching assignments nor the assignment to write God's songs was financially beneficial. I did not want income from these. They were the result of spiritual gifts I received upon being born again. I knew better than to expect any payment for the work assignments I took on for our amazing Father.

My latest assignment was to write what I thought would be just one book about comparing God's holy words, the scriptures, with the current trends in our culture. I knew we were headed in the wrong direction, and God saw this as well. He guided me and corrected my writing every step of the way. I often wrote sentences which I knew conveyed the thoughts I was receiving from God. However, He would stop me and have me back out the words I used in favor of words which He inspired. They seemed to say the same thing, but God knows how to use just the right words which He directs to be written.

I have always had a close relationship with God the Father, God the Son, and God the Holy Spirit. I could feel deep inside what they wanted. Sometimes this included an image or words and a telepathic message which matched the image.

I received training as what I eventually realized was because I was God ordained. As part of this training, God guided me to attend and even join various different churches of different denominations. I know that the reason for this was for me to observe both the differences and similarities between denominations. I also was instructed to join, as a member, a nondenominational church. That training which I received allowed me to understand that the various denominations, which were created by man, not God, need to agree that they disagree on certain things. However, they should be trying their best to agree to concentrate on those things in which they do agree.

People are confused by the bickering and arguing that goes on with the various denominations. They tend to not go to church because if the biblical scholars are unable to agree, then how can they be expected to agree.

Helen "Darlene" (Jones) Vietmeier
Born: May 14, 1945 (Mother's Day)
Died: January 6, 2013
Married: Raymond H. Vietmeier February 1, 1964

Raymond Junior McDowell
Born: September 19, 1943
Still Living
Adopted: August 1948 By: Irvin and Bernice Vietmeier
Renamed: Raymond Harry Vietmeier
Married: Helen "Darlene" Jones February 1, 1964

Children: Michael Raymond Vietmeier Born June 30, 1969
Mary Ann (Vietmeier) Davis born December 2, 1972

Marraige of Helen "Darlene" Jones and Raymond
Harry Vietmeier February 1, 1964